For Children in Grades 2-6

Empowering
Children of
Incarcerated Parents

{
by
Stacey Burgess, LCSW
Tonia Caselman, PhD, LCSW
Jennifer Carsey, MSW
}

youth light
inc.

© 2009 by YouthLight, Inc. | Chapin, SC 29036

Layout and Design by Melody Sandola
Project Editing by Susan Bowman

Library of Congress Control Number
2009930067

ISBN
978-1-59850-076-9

10 9 8 7 6 5 4 3 2 1
Printed in the United States

TABLE OF CONTENTS

About the Authors

Stacey Burgess, LCSW, is a Licensed Clinical Social Worker currently providing mental health services in a public elementary school in Tulsa, Oklahoma. She specializes with at-risk children living in poverty, many of whom are children of incarcerated parents. Stacey has a background in Child Welfare, and currently provides training for foster and adoptive parents. She enjoys incorporating humor and activity into her practice.

Tonia Caselman, PhD, LCSW, is an Associate Professor at the University of Oklahoma. She also maintains a private practice where she specializes in children and families. She is the author/co-author of several journal articles and books, including *Impulse Control for Elementary Students, Impulse Control for Middle Schoolers, Boundaries,* and *Empathy: The Social Emotion.* She is also co-author of several therapeutic games, including *The Impulse Control Game, Remote Control Impulse Control,* and *Boundaries Baseball.*

Jennifer Carsey, MSW, currently works in Child Welfare as a Family Group Conferencing Facilitator. She has experience working with families and children in crisis particularly in the areas of addiction and trauma/abuse. She uses a systemic, solution-focused approach in her practice.

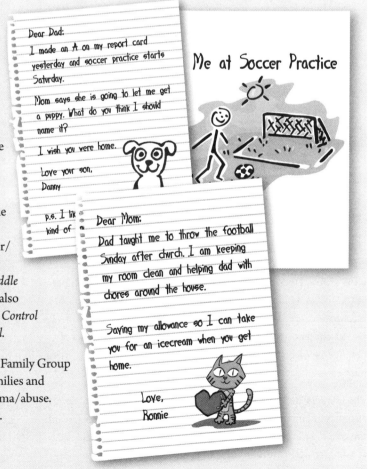

3

Introduction

An increasing number of children face the incarceration of a parent. Children of these prisoners are an invisible population. No one agency is directly responsible for them, and schools are often unaware a student has an incarcerated parent. Statistics show the number of people in prison quadrupled between 1980 and 2001 (Phillips, Burns, Wagner, Kramer & Robbins, 2002; Travis, 2004). Of those currently in a state prison, 55 percent reported having at least one child under the age of 18 (Travis, 2005). This translates to an estimated 1.5-2 million children that are affected nationwide; approximately 1 in 50 children have a parent who is incarcerated (Miller, 2006; Phillips et al., 2002). This represents 2 percent of all minor children and 7 percent of all African-American children (Mumola, 2000). If history of prior incarceration is analyzed, the number of children affected jumps an additional 10 million (Miller, 2006). These statistics suggest children of incarcerated parents are a sizeable at-risk population within the United States.

Compounding the issue of parental incarceration is the likelihood these children lived with multiple risk factors prior to the parents' arrests. Research indicates children of incarcerated parents have been exposed to crime, poverty, family substance abuse, violence, and other criminal behavior (Johnson & Waldfogel, 2002; Miller, 2006). In fact, a recent study found that among children in the child welfare system, those with incarcerated parents were exposed to a greater number of problems than other children in the system (Phillips & Gleeson, 2007). Furthermore, a parent's incarceration adds to these environmental risk factors a ruptured parent-child bond, an altered support system, and the stigma of parental incarceration. It may also force the child to adjust to living with an extended family member or in foster care (Travis, 2005).

The financial burden that often accompanies the arrest of a parent also plays a large role in the child's life. For instance, in 1997, seven out of ten parents in state prisons stated they had been employed at least part-time immediately preceding their incarceration (Mumola, 2000). The effects of the diminished flow of income can be felt differently. In two parent families, the non-imprisoned parent must make up for the lost income. If the incarcerated parent is the sole provider for the children, extended family members might care for the child in the parent's absence, but the burden of another mouth to feed often places additional strain on this family unit. This is a frequently encountered scenario since 79 percent of children live with a relative when a parent is incarcerated (Mumola, 2000). Additionally, the number of incarcerated mothers grew 87 percent from 1991 to 2000 (Mumola, 2000). As more women are incarcerated, more children will experience the disruption of having an absent parent and possibly alternate living arrangements.

The symptoms children of incarcerated parents present are varied. Children can display internalizing behaviors, such as depression, anxiety, and attachment difficulties, or they can display externalizing behaviors, such as disruptive or delinquent behavior (Travis, 2005). Feelings of anger, fear, guilt, grief, rejection, shame, and loneliness are also common (Gabel, 1992; Greene, Haney, & Hurtado, 2000). Lifelong consequences can be seen in the fact that children of incarcerated parents are 5-6 times more likely than their peers to enter the criminal justice system themselves (Miller, 2006). The cyclical nature of intergenerational incarceration highlights the need for special attention and effective treatment for this vulnerable group of children.

Using this Book

Empowering Children of Incarcerated Parents is designed to be used with either individual children or with groups of children who have an incarcerated parent. There are advantages and disadvantages to both individual sessions and group sessions. While it may be helpful for children to meet in groups so they can know there are others who have had similar experiences, it may be difficult to identify these children as many of them have learned how to hide this information and have found other ways to explain their parents' absences. Groups can provide support and reduce stigma, but individual sessions can be tailored to an individual child's specific needs. Typically, children whose parents are incarcerated have strong desires for privacy (Nesmith & Ruhland, 2008). The authors suggest serious consideration be given to how the content of this manual is delivered.

The content of *Empowering Children of Incarcerated Parents* has been purposefully and intentionally developed based on a thorough literature review. Each lesson is based on empirical findings and/or recommendations by experts in the field. It is also recommended that informed consents from caregivers be obtained prior to working with children. *Empowering Children of Incarcerated Parents* is honest and direct about incarceration issues, and caregivers may not have disclosed some of this information to their child.

Each lesson includes the following sections: Notes to Facilitator, a Script, Prison Letters (between a fictional boy and his incarcerated father), Discussion Questions, Activities and Reproducible Worksheets. The Notes to Facilitator provide a description of that lesson's topic and describe the evidenced-based practices for that particular problem. The authors have made every attempt to identify solid research with children of incarcerated parents as participants. When those studies were not available, other relevant research was examined. All subsequent activities and worksheets are based on this literature review. In addition, suggestions are provided for out-of-session activities. A script is also provided for facilitators to read to the children as an introduction to each lesson. This script can also be adapted and summarized as needed.

The Prison Letters found in each chapter are examples of correspondence between a son and his incarcerated father. These letters can be read with or to children during sessions. After each letter there are several discussion questions to help the child connect her/his own thoughts and feelings to Alonzo's story. These narratives are based on the idea that, "The right story told to the right person(s) at the right time in the right way can powerfully define and shape both individuals and the systems into which they organize themselves" (Franz, 1995). Alonzo's story provides points of connection for the children. In these stories Alonzo's father shows insight and wisdom into the situation. He says the right things to Alonzo at the right times. We cannot expect each child's parent to always know the words to say. It is our hope as children hear the words of affirmation and encouragement from Alonzo's father, they will be able to internalize some of these messages for themselves as well. Finally, the letters provide children with an example of how to keep connected to their incarcerated parent and may give them ideas about the kinds of information they can share with their parent through letter writing. Indeed, research suggests incarcerated parents are concerned about their children's academic and social/emotional development (Kazura, 2001) and children benefit when incarcerated parents assist with their coping skills development (Mazza, 2002).

The Discussion Questions give children thinking questions relevant and applicable to each topic. They provide a segue to activities and worksheets. They help children to be actively engaged in the introduction of new information and to process past events, thoughts, feelings, behaviors, etc., as well as consider new thoughts and behaviors. Discussion questions can help children organize their thoughts, better understand what has happened to them, and develop additional sources of resilience. For children who are auditory learners, it is particularly important to incorporate small-group discussions, listening, and verbal interpretations.

> **Lifelong consequences can be seen in the fact that children of incarcerated parents are 5-6 times more likely than their peers to enter the criminal justice system themselves.**

The Activities section describes tasks, games, and role plays to help children practice concepts and skills so they are not simply intellectualizing information. Many counselors who work with children find that therapeutic activities are more effective than simple "talk" therapies. The Activities tap into some of the more expressive therapies, such as game play, visualization, art therapy, music therapy, psychodrama, etc. Therapeutic activities benefit both children who have a difficult time expressing themselves with words and those who overly express themselves with words. Therapeutic activities are particularly effective for kinesthetic learners who need to move, touch, and do in order to better learn new concepts.

Finally, Reproducible Worksheets are provided. These pages will give children a visual modality to reflect, identify, and develop self-awareness and coping skills. Children may not always be able to explain how they think, feel, and act, but by using the Worksheets, they can be prompted to consider various concepts in order to better understand themselves and their situations. Visual learners need to see words, pictures, timelines, etc., to maximize their learning. The inclusion of Discussion Questions, Activities, and Worksheets reaches every child's learning style, whether it be auditory, kinesthetic, or visual.

Mazza (2006) also highlights the importance of remembering that while these are children with incarcerated parents, they are also just children. Therefore, it is important to have fun and be playful. Other suggestions for facilitators include:

» Use (or encourage caregivers to use) inspirational stories or videos showcasing characters overcoming hardships. Some examples are *The Karate Kid*, *The Lion King*, *Free Willy*, and *The Tortoise and the Hare*. Biographies of real people who have overcome obstacles are also recommended. Some of these include biographies of Martin Luther King, Frederick Douglas, Amelia Earhart, Albert Einstein, Harriet Tubman, Helen Keller, Hank Aaron, and many others. When reading/watching these stories and biographies, draw parallels between the protagonists and the child.

» Rephrase negative statements to show empathy (identifying feelings), but offer hope that is reality-based. For example, if the child says, "No one wants to play with me," respond with, "It's lonely when you can't find someone to play with, but I remember you and Jeremy had a great time at recess the other day."

» Repeat proverbs, old sayings, or expressions that are easy to remember to instill hope and tenacity. Some examples might be, "If at first you don't succeed, try, try again" and "Every cloud has a silver lining" and "I think I can; I think I can."

» Celebrate successes and catch the child doing things right. Be exuberant about these! Praise!

» Help children recognize helpful and unhelpful thoughts. Teach and encourage them to use the helpful thoughts (no "stinkin' thinkin'"!)

» If children become overwhelmed by their feelings or their interactions with one another (if facilitating a group), teach and coach the Turtle Technique. In this technique the counselor encourages children to imagine themselves as turtles. They can withdraw into their shells (i.e., pull their arms and legs in close to their bodies, put their head down, and close their eyes). During this time the counselor can use soothing language or progressive muscle relaxation to help calm emotional tensions.

» Finally, there are several children's books that focus on incarcerated parents. It may be helpful to use some of these in sessions. These include:

» *My Daddy's in Jail* by Janet Bender

» *What is Jail, Mommy* by Jackie Stanglin

» *Visiting Day* by Jacqueline Woodson

» *A Visit to the Big House* by Oliver Butterworth

» *I Know How You Feel Because This Happened to Me* Center for Children with Incarcerated Parents,

» *Mama Loves Me from Away* by Pat Brisson

» *Joey's Visit* by Donna Jones

» *My Mother and I Are Growing Strong*er by Inez Maury

» *When Andy's Father Went to Prison* by Martha Whitmore Hickman

» *Let's Talk About When Your Parent Is in Jail* by Maureen K. Wittbold

» *There Are Some Real Special Kids In Our Class* by Frank M. Black

» *Keeping in Touch by Long Distance* by Ann Kerniski

» *A Visit with Daddy* by Frank M. Black

» *A Visit with Mommy* by Frank M. Black

» *My Mom Went to Jail* by Kathleen Hodgkins and Suzanne Bergen

» *Dad's in Prison* by Sandra Cain and Margaret Speed

Background and Needs for Children of Incarcerated Parents

The needs of children with incarcerated parents are complex and numerous. This book is not intended to singularly meet all the needs of these vulnerable children. Additional services are needed. The following interventions should be considered when working with individual children of incarcerated parents.

First, research shows these children and their families are often isolated and live in poverty (Nesmith & Ruhland, 2008). It is suggested that those using this book may also need to solicit the help of social workers/case managers and broker other additional services, such as financial resources, mentors, tutors, parenting skills programs, etc. It may be important to advocate for and assist in the arrangements for visitation and comprehensive family programs. Finally, it may even be helpful to contact the incarcerated parent in order to update her/him on issues concerning her/his child(ren) and counsel them on how they can play a part in their children's lives. Of course, it is important to obtain consent from the child's guardian prior to doing this.

» Children of incarcerated parents often find themselves living in poverty before and/or after the incarceration. These families of prisoners are often poorly connected to human services. We suggest readers assess the physical needs of these children and make appropriate referrals for assistance, such as the Supplemental Nutrition Assistance Program (formerly known as food stamps), groceries, utility assistance, housing assistance, holiday assistance, etc.

» Visitation between children and their incarcerated parent is often very minimal despite the fact that children who maintain contact with their parent may exhibit fewer internalizing and externalizing behaviors (Sack, Seidler, & Thomas, 1976; Stanton, 1980) and have better long-term outcomes (Edin, Nelson, & Paranal, 2004; Klein, Bartholomew, & Hibbert, 2002; La Vigne, Naser, Brooks, & Castro, 2005). While it is recognized the distance between a child's home and the prison is a key contributor to visitation (or lack thereof), readers are encouraged to support and facilitate phone conversations and visits between children and parents in whatever ways they can.

» When asked directly, children of incarcerated parents have difficulty identifying role models (Nesmith & Ruhland, 2008). Indeed, many states have identified the need for mentoring programs for this vulnerable population. We suggest readers find local programs offering mentors to at-risk children. The U.S. Administration for Children, Youth, and Families fund programs such as Big Brothers/Big Sisters, Volunteers of America, and the Salvation Army, and many community schools also have mentoring programs. If these are unavailable or there is a prohibitive waiting list, we suggest the reader create a partnership with a relevant agency and possibly write a grant to establish a mentoring program for children of incarcerated parents (see http://www.acf.hhs.gov/programs/fbci/progs/fbci_mcp.)

» Children of incarcerated parents often have difficulty performing well in school. The reasons for this may vary from learning disabilities/ADHD to frequent moves and changes in schools to trauma-related concentration problems. Whatever the reason, children of incarcerated parents can benefit from tutoring and additional assistance with school work. Advocacy with classroom teachers may result in extra time given to the child, including before and after school assistance. Referral to a Title I reading program may also be helpful. In addition, many schools have community partners of individuals to read and tutor students.

» Children of incarcerated parents who show a high degree of resilience are those who are involved in extracurricular activities (Nesmith & Ruhland, 2008). We suggest readers assist children in identifying their interests (or potential interests) and assist them to engage in extracurricular activities that foster those interests. Examples of activities might be sports, church, music, theatre, art, Scouts, etc.

» If caregivers are family members, children of incarcerated parents are often hypersensitive to the caregivers' stresses and emotions (Nesmith & Ruhland, 2008). This compounds the children's existing worry for the parent who is incarcerated. In situations where the caregiver has a poor relationship with the incarcerated parent, children feel worried in both directions, often feeling the need to hide or understate their concerns for both. We suggest readers allow children to speak openly about their worries and fears about parents and caregivers and/or make appropriate referrals to counselors or social workers.

» Children of incarcerated parents experience stigma and shame of their incarcerated parent. Stigma is a major obstacle for intervention. Educating the public regarding the needs and plight of children of incarcerated parents can help reduce stigma. Providing information to teachers, physicians, churches, and to the public through newspaper, TV, and radio campaigns can help children to avoid feeling inferior.

Lastly, the San Francisco Partnership for Incarcerated Parents has published a Bill of Rights for children of incarcerated parents. Readers are encouraged to download this brochure from http://www.fcnetwork.org/billofrights.pdf and share it with caregivers, teachers, counselors, mentors, and other significant adults. A summary of the recommendations include:

» A child should be told the truth about his/her parent's status. (While this may be optimal, caution should be taken to ensure permission is given for this disclosure. Ideally, primary caregivers should be encouraged to explain a parent's incarceration.)

» A child should be heard without judgment.

» A child should be offered the companionship of others who share similar circumstances so s/he does not feel alone (again, with caregiver consent).

» A child should have contact with his/her parent and to have that relationship recognized and valued.

» A child should never be stigmatized for the actions of his/her parent and should always be treated with respect and as a person of worth and potential.

Lesson 1
Understanding What Happened

Notes to Facilitator

Children have an intense need to understand the world around them. For some children a parent's arrest can spark a chain of events they have no control over, and research has indicated the emotional distress of children may be intensified by the unwillingness of family, friends, or caregivers to discuss the parent's incarceration (Snyder-Joy & Carlo, 1998). Though adults try to shelter children from the ugliness of the situation, this often has an inverse effect upon their emotional well-being. Moreover, there is often limited opportunity for children of incarcerated parents to obtain correct and unbiased information about her/his parents' incarcerations (Nesmith & Ruhland, 2008).

Circumstances surrounding the parent's arrest also can have lasting emotional consequences. Approximately one out of five children of incarcerated parents witnesses the parent's arrest. The effects of this cannot be understated (Johnston, 2001). Children who witness their mother's arrest, for example, often suffer nightmares and flashbacks of the arrest incident (Kampfner, 1995). Similarly, the abrupt and unexpected changes surrounding the parent's arrest can have the effect of multiple traumas on children as they witness the forcible removal of their parent from the home, lose the caregiver and protector they have known, and often must move to a different location away from the home they know (Kampfner, 1995).

Children who do not personally witness the arrest are still profoundly affected. For example, children who are in school at the time of the arrest may return to an empty residence and be unaware of what happened. Also, children may have expected to visit with a noncustodial parent on a particular day and then not understand why s/he did not show up.

> **Approximately one out of five children of incarcerated parents witnesses the parent's arrest.**

Children are often intentionally deceived "for their own good" about their parents' incarcerations (Mazza, 2002). Children may be told their fathers have moved away or their whereabouts are unknown. This may increase the child's sense of abandonment, which can lead to anger, anxiety, shame, and depression. Short-term effects of parental arrest can include an array of traumatic stress reactions (Kampfner, 1995), and long-term effects can include a distrust of the police and the courts as well as unwillingness to look to law enforcement for protection (Stanton, 1980).

While each child's experience of his/her parent's arrest and incarceration is unique, children benefit from having developmentally-appropriate information so they do not form their own erroneous conclusions about what has happened or what will happen in the future. In the absence of correct information, children often use their imaginations to "fill in the missing pieces" (Nesmith & Ruhland, 2008). While there may be valid reasons for secrecy (e.g., jobs, welfare payments, child custody, housing, etc.,

being in jeopardy), children need to understand what has happened to their families and to be able to talk about their experiences. In fact, families who were open and honest about discussing difficult topics showed improved social and academic outcomes (Marin, Bohanek, & Fivush, 2008). The more a child's caretakers are able to talk about the incarcerated parent, the more comfortable the child will be discussing his/her parent and the feelings surrounding their incarceration.

Suggestions:

» Encourage caregivers to be honest (in a developmentally appropriate way) with children regarding their parent's incarceration. Likewise, encourage children to ask questions about their parents when they feel confused.

» Provide children's books regarding parental incarceration to both caregivers and children.

» Children may not understand how long their parent is going to be away. Explain to them this depends on what law was broken, if the parent has been in jail/prison before, and the way s/he acts in jail/prison.

» States and individual jails/prisons vary on visitation practices. It is reassuring to children to know how they can communicate with their parents while they are in jail/prison. Help children and caregivers obtain information regarding visitation, telephone calls, letter writing, etc.

Script

Did you know there are many children in the United States with parents in jail or prison? You are not alone in going through this difficult time in your family. Many times when a parent goes to jail, the kids have to go live with grandparents or other adults who can take care of them. Other times they stay with the other parent, but many things in their life may change. People go to jail or prison for breaking laws. This is a consequence for breaking rules like kids having to go to time-out or getting grounded when they get in trouble. Usually police take people to jail for breaking laws, and then a court made up of judges, lawyers, and other people decide how long that person will have to stay in jail. When a parent goes to jail, it is never the child's fault. Many times kids can stay in touch with their parent in prison by writing letters or even visiting. It is normal to have confusing feelings when something difficult happens in your family. A good thing you can do to help you through this time is talk about your feelings with people you trust and ask questions when there are things you are wondering about or do not understand.

Prison Letters

Alonzo is an 11 year-old-boy whose father recently went to jail for selling drugs. Alonzo was at home when the police came and picked up his father. He cried on the front porch as his father was taken away. Alonzo lives with his mother most of the time. She has problems with depression, and when she is feeling really bad, Alonzo and his siblings go and stay with his grandma. Alonzo has two older sisters and one older brother. Soon after Alonzo's dad went to jail, Alonzo got his first letter.

Dear Alonzo,

I am sorry about what you had to see last week. I guess you know now the police found out I was selling some stuff. I could lie and tell you that I didn't do anything wrong, but I did. Now I have to face the consequences for my choices. I have a lawyer, she seems like a good lady, and she is going to help me. Next I go to court, and the judge will tell me then how long I have to stay in jail. I am hoping I will be home soon, but we will have to see what happens.

Here I have my own bed, and I share a sink and a toilet in a room with another guy. We get to watch TV, read in the library, and play basketball outside sometimes. Everybody here has to wear the same kind of clothes. There are guards who tell us what to do. I don't like being told what to do, but when I do it, I get treated better. It's pretty boring, and I wish I were home. I am sorry for what I have done to our family. I wish I never got mixed up with drugs. They ruin people's lives. I just wish I could take it all back. Stay away from drugs, Son, whatever you do. They will only lead to trouble. You are smart. I am proud of your good grades. The fact that I can't be with you right now does not change my love for you. I think about you and our family every minute. What is happening to us is not your fault. Make sure you try and find things to do that make you happy, and write me when you can. I am and will always be your daddy.

Love, Dad

Questions:

1. What are consequences?

2. What do you imagine jail to be like?

3. What was the consequence for Alonzo's dad selling drugs?

4. What do you think will be different about Alonzo's relationship with his dad? What will be the same?

Additional Discussion Questions

» When was the last time you saw your parent?

» What were you told when your parent was sent to jail? How did you feel?

» What is something you'd like to know about your parent's arrest?

» Do you know how long your parent will be in jail?

» How are things in your life the same as before your parent went to jail? How are they different? What do you miss the most?

Activities
{Get to Know You Game}

Objective: To become acquainted with the child(ren) and to develop rapport

Have the child take a handful of M&Ms® from a bag, but instruct him/her not to eat them until the game is finished. Separate the M&Ms® by color.

» For each red M&M®, have the child tell you something s/he likes to do for fun.

» For each brown M&M®, have the child tell you something about his/her school.

» For each yellow M&M®, have the child tell you something about his/her family.

» For each green M&M®, have the child tell you something about his/her incarcerated parent.

For group activity, have each child take an M&M® and tell the group something for each one s/he took.

{True or False Game}

Objective: To help the child(ren) begin to express and normalize feelings about a parent's incarceration

Write the words True, False, and Unsure each on a separate piece of paper. Tape the papers to the wall in three different places in the room. Read the following statements and have the child go and stand by the word s/he thinks best fits how s/he feels about the statement.

1. Everyone who goes to jail is a bad person.

2. People go to jail for breaking laws.

3. If my family member goes to jail, I will probably end up in jail someday.

4. I will never see my family member who is in jail again.

5. It is ok to enjoy my life even though I have a family member in jail.

6. My family member in jail does not think about me.

7. No one else has gone through the same things I am going through right now.

8. It is normal to miss my family member who is in jail and feel sad about what happened.

9. There are people who care about what I am going through.

10. I have to keep the fact my parent is in jail a secret from most people.

11. If my family member really loved me, they would not have gone to jail.

12. I could have done something to stop my family member from going to jail.

13. Police are there to help people and keep them safe.

14. I should try and keep in contact with my parent that is in jail.

15. I can't let my caregiver see me cry.

For group activity, have the children each chose their own answer. Encourage the children to be honest in their answers and not just answer a certain way because the other kids are.

Follow-up: Discuss the child(ren)'s reaction to the activity. If done in a group, ask children how it feels to see that others had similar feelings.

{Consider the Consequences}

Objective: To explore the concept of consequences and connect incarceration with consequences for breaking laws

Have the child explore consequences by reading the following scenarios in which a person has a choice between doing and not doing an action. Discuss reasons why the child should and should not do the action, and then have the child make a choice about what s/he would do.

For group activity, have three children sit side by side. The child in the middle will read the scenario. The child on the right side should try and tell him/her why s/he should choose to do the action, and the child on the left side will try and tell him/her reasons not to do the action. Have the child in the middle choose whether or not to do the action.

For example, Child A says, "You should steal it because you are hungry and you won't get caught." Child B says, "Don't do it, you might get in trouble, and they could call the police."

Scenario 1: Alex is at the grocery store and he is very hungry. He doesn't have any money, but he doesn't think anyone is watching, and he could probably get away with stealing a candy bar.

Scenario 2: Yarissa goes into her bedroom and finds her new Barbie has a new haircut. Yarissa runs to her brother's room planning to break his new toy truck.

Scenario 3: Amir knows the answer to the question his teacher just asked and is raising his hand. Amir doesn't understand why the teacher isn't calling on him and wants to just yell out the answer.

Scenario 4: Jackie is tired of Mica always making fun of her. She decides the next time Mica says something to her, she will probably just punch her in the face.

Follow-up: Discuss with the child(ren) how every action has a consequence. Ask her/him to share personal behaviors that have brought negative consequences. Then give her/him the opportunity to discuss the behavior that gave his/her parent the consequence of jail or prison. (This last part should be optional. No child should be forced to share if s/he is uncomfortable.)

{What's Changed}

Objective: To identify how life has changed since a parent went to prison

Fold a piece of paper in half and ask the child to draw on one half of the paper a picture of what his/her family was like before his/her parent went to prison. On the other half of the piece of paper, ask him/her to draw what his/her family is like now.

For group activity, give an opportunity for the children to share their pictures with the group. Look for commonalities between group members about the changes that have occurred.

Follow-up: Discuss additional ways his/her family is the same and ways it is different.

{Staying Connected}

Objective: To help the child(ren) maintain connections with the incarcerated parent (making sure that this is OK with the primary caregiver)

Have the child write a letter to her/his incarcerated parent. Some children may never have done this before, even if their parent has already been away for a long time. Explain to the child how to start a letter, encourage her/him to ask questions, tell about his/her daily life, discuss any good news, draw a picture, etc. You may want to provide the child with an envelope and stamp. Teach the child how to address the envelope. Children may need assistance in locating an address for their incarcerated parents. This information can be found on the Department of Corrections website in most states.

For group activity, have the group write letters together. Give children the opportunity to share their letters or pictures with the group.

Follow-up: Discuss any problems that the child(ren) has had in staying in touch with her/his parent. Brainstorm solutions for these problems.

Reproducible Worksheets

Reproducible Worksheet 1.1, *Understanding What Happened*, helps children to see the correlation between rules (something they are familiar with) and laws (something they may not be familiar with). The worksheet asks them to identify some rules they have to follow and to circle the kinds of consequences they experience when they do not follow rules. It then asks if they know what law(s) their parent broke and how they found out. This worksheet (and any resultant conversations) should not be used to add shame but, rather, to make sense of what has happened and empower children to work out any concerns.

Reproducible Worksheet 1.2, *The Purpose of Laws*, helps children to see that laws are meant for (1) keeping people safe, (2) keeping property safe, (3) keeping the community peaceful and orderly, and (4) creating fairness. They are asked to examine a list of laws and match them with their purpose. Because children of incarcerated parents may have developed some mistrust for law enforcement and the law in general, this worksheet can be helpful in assisting them understand the purpose of laws.

Reproducible Worksheet 1.3, *Understanding What is Happening*, helps children to consider all of the activities their parent may be engaged in while incarcerated. Helping children to understand these concrete activities may assist in dispelling any fears they may have about their parents' environments.

Reproducible Worksheet 1.4, *Wordsearch*, instructs children to find various words they may hear over and over related to their parents' incarcerations. This gives them the opportunity to become more desensitized to the use of these words and also to ask facilitators the meaning of any words they do not fully understand.

Reproducible Worksheet 1.5, *Definitions*, uses a multiple choice format instructing children to find the appropriate definition of words they may have heard (e.g., arrest, hearing, sentence, felony, trial, lawyer and courts). Again, giving children real information can help them avoid filling in their knowledge voids with erroneous and anxiety-producing material.

Reproducible 1.1

Understanding What Happened

Children have rules. When children break rules, they can get into trouble. What are some rules that you have to follow?

1. _____

2. _____

3. _____

What are some of things that happen to you when you do not follow the rules? Circle the consequences that you have experienced from not following rules:

Put in time-out   Wrote sentences   Did extra chores   Got a spanking
                         repeatedly

Couldn't watch   Sent to the   Listened to a lecture
TV or play with   principal's office
video games

        Went to bed early   Couldn't play with a
                                                   favorite toy

Grown-ups have rules, too. These are called laws. Sometimes when grown-ups don't obey laws, they get in trouble. They are told to pay fines (money to the court) or are sent to jail or prison. Jail and prison are like long time-outs for adults. Do you know what law your parent broke?

_____

How did you find out that your parent was going to go to jail or prison?

_____

_____

The Purpose of Laws

Laws keep the community peaceful and orderly. They are written to keep people and their belongings safe. Look at the laws written on the left and match them to their purpose (reason they were written) on the right by drawing a line. The first one is done for you.

Wear a seatbelt when riding in a car.

Stop the car when you see a red light.

No one can go onto someone else's property without her/his permission.

Do not play music too loudly.

No one can be refused a job based on her/his gender or race.

Do not write on statues that are part of parks and buildings.

Do not take things from a store that do not belong to you.

Do not hit, push, kick, or hurt someone else in any way.

All children have the right to a free and public education.

To keep people safe

To protect people's belongings and property

To keep things as fair as possible

To keep the neighborhood or community peaceful and attractive

Understanding What is Happening Now

When grown-ups are in jail or prison, they are required to work. Do you know what job your parent has?

_____

_____

People in jail or prison also have free time to read, watch TV, walk and jog, exercise, work on hobbies, or go to special counseling classes. Do you know what your parent does in her/his spare time?

_____

_____

Sometimes people in jail or prison can go to school or take parenting classes. Do you know if your parent is taking any kind of classes? If s/he is, do you know what kind of classes they are?

_____

_____

Prisons and jails have doctors and nurses around if they are needed. Do you know if your parent has received any health care while s/he has been away?

_____

_____

Prisons and jails also have ministers and church services available. Do you know if your parent has seen a minister or has gone to church services?

_____

_____

Do you have any worries about your parent's life in jail or prison? What are they?

_____

_____

Wordsearch

Circle the following words:

TRIAL	ARREST	LAWYER	POLICE
COURT	JAIL	PRISON	HEARING
LEGAL	SENTENCE	CUSTODY	FELONY

```
Y  G  F  Z  M  Y  J  A  I  L  W  B  U  F  L
B  P  E  W  L  E  G  A  L  Q  B  L  W  V  A
N  O  L  R  P  K  A  I  W  G  E  Q  D  D  W
P  W  O  G  V  Q  J  N  N  J  F  S  E  P  Y
U  R  N  G  L  I  O  I  Z  S  C  H  C  C  E
A  P  Y  A  D  S  R  X  T  E  U  U  N  Q  R
H  X  V  K  I  A  O  A  G  N  S  R  A  J  X
O  H  T  R  E  R  C  O  U  T  T  E  L  W  N
U  W  P  H  D  R  X  G  T  E  O  T  X  R  W
U  P  K  H  J  E  E  L  F  N  D  R  O  W  F
I  G  O  X  L  S  O  G  B  C  Y  I  Y  I  D
I  I  N  L  A  T  Q  P  N  E  W  A  E  V  V
F  F  M  W  I  R  O  D  O  M  J  L  A  H  K
U  O  I  R  Q  C  U  S  K  A  K  P  X  K  I
K  L  Y  I  J  S  E  F  W  M  C  O  U  R  T
```

Definitions

Circle the correct definition of each of the words listed below:

1. Arrest
    a. A place to rest or relax
    b. When the police pick up someone who has broken the law
    c. Leftovers after a big meal

2. Hearing
    a. A ringing sound that is here
    b. Jewelry worn on the ears
    c. A court case that is heard by a judge

3. Sentence
    a. Punishment for breaking a law
    b. Sending someone on an errand
    c. Feeling tense or stressed out

4. Trial
    a. Trying over and over again
    b. Three things stuck together
    c. A court case that goes before a judge and sometimes before a group of people called a jury

5. Felony
    a. A crime or law-breaking activity
    b. To fall on the letter 'Y'
    c. To look like a cat or feline

6. Lawyer
    a. Someone who sings, "La, la, la"
    b. Someone who goes to court and gives people advice about the law
    c. Someone who mows lawns

7. Court
    a. A rope
    b. Two people who hurt each other
    c. A place where judges and lawyers meet to do business about people based on the law

Lesson 2
Building a Support System

Notes to Facilitator

Developing a strong support system is critical in helping children cope with their parents' incarcerations. Children who feel they have little social support have a greater incidence of externalizing problems ("Children of Incarcerated Parents," 2007). When a parent is removed from a child's life, it forces the child to adjust to altered support systems. This can include a move, a different family formation and/or foster care (Travis, 2005). Not surprisingly, in 1997, it was estimated 10.7 percent of children living with their grandparents had incarcerated parents (Johnson & Waldfogel, 2002).

Social support has long been recognized as an important component of healthy adaptation and development; for example, social support has been identified in improving adolescent depression (Barrera & Garrison-Jones, 1992), improving academic performance (Dubow, Tisak, Causey, & Hryshko, 1991; Ford & Sutphen, 1996), and reducing delinquent behaviors (Zigler, Taussig, & Black, 1992). The literature on resiliency factors also clearly identifies the primacy of family, peer, teacher, and community support in predicting positive outcomes for children (Benard, 1991; Bogenschneider, 1996; Richman & Bowen, 1997). There is also evidence that close emotional relationships with extended family may lessen the negative effects of parent incarceration (Bloom & Steinhart, 1993 as cited in Parke & Clarke-Stewart, 2001).

In creating additional social support for at-risk youth, research has found mentoring helps to improve academic performance, social behavior, relationships and decision making skills in children (Grossman & Garry, 1997). One study found that when compared to controls, children who participated in the Big Brothers/Big Sisters mentoring program were significantly less likely to initiate drug use or consume alcohol; the effect was even stronger among minority youth (Grossman & Garry, 1997). The role of a caring adult serves as a protective factor for children, especially when a relationship is developed that provides a supportive role model over a long period of time (Pelco & Reed-Victor, 2007). Children who feel abandoned by a parent will do better with a mentor who can make a long term commitment (Mazza, 2002).

> **Children who feel abandoned by a parent will do better with a mentor who can make a long term commitment.**

To help fight the social stigma experienced by these children, it is important for them to know there are others who share their same thoughts and feelings. Group work can not only provide additional social support, it can provide opportunities for children to share their feelings about their parents' incarcerations (Mazza, 2002).

Suggestions:

» Encourage caregivers to spend additional quality time with children. For fun activities to share with caregivers, see Appendix A, on page 95.

» Suggest to school counselors and principals that children of incarcerated parents be placed with sensitive, relationship-oriented teachers.

» Encourage positive connections to churches, synagogues and mosques where children can feel connected to both peers and adults.

» Refer and match children with mentors. Many agencies provide mentors. The most successful mentoring programs focus on developing trusting relationships and social skills (rather than focusing on behavioral goals, such as improving grades or decreasing drug abuse) and last at least one year (Herrera, Sipe, & McClanahan, 2000). Big Brothers/Big Sisters is one example of a mentoring program.

» Develop (or encourage school teachers and counselors to develop) curricula that addresses growing up in special circumstances – including the circumstance of families where there is an incarcerated member. This will help children feel more accepted.

» Develop small support groups for children of incarcerated parents and their families.

Script

A lot of kids who have a parent go to jail or prison feel lonely or like no one understands or cares what they are going through. This is not true. The truth is there are other kids going through the same type of thing you are. There are also people who care about what you think and how you feel. Finding people you can trust to talk about your feelings will help you. These people might be counselors, teachers, grandparents, friends, or other people. Sometimes kids who have a parent in prison feel embarrassed about what happened to their family. It is normal to feel this way, but not everyone will think badly about you because of your parent's mistakes. Many kids have families with problems. Remember it is OK to ask people for help when you need it.

Prison Letters

"Dear Dad,

I miss you a lot. I think about you and what happened all the time. It seems like you have already been gone forever. Is prison scary? Do people fight there? Are you going to dig a tunnel and escape? Things at home have been kind of hard, but I am doing OK. Mom has been crying a lot. She says she does not know how we can pay the rent now. She stayed in her room all day yesterday. Grandma has been coming over every day. She helps with telling us to clean our rooms and cooking for us when Mom is feeling bad. Last week Mom went to school and told Ms. Wells what happened. Mom cried again while they were talking. Ms. Wells is really nice to me. She lets me come in her office if I finish my work, and we play checkers. She is really bad at checkers because I always win. She also told me she is going to find a man to be my mentor. He will come and hang out with me once a week and even bring me lunch. I am glad Ms. Wells knows what happened. It makes me feel better that it is not a secret from everyone. She told me it is ok to talk about being sad, but it is still embarrassing. I do worry about you a lot. I hope no one hurts you there. Ms. Wells says she will try and help us go to visit you. She also says it is important she and I make sure there are lots of people to give me extra love and hugs while you are gone. Do you think it is ok for me to do all that stuff? I don't want you to get mad at me for having fun while you are stuck in jail. I like it when you write me letters. I will draw you a picture. I hope you can hang it on your wall.

I love you Dad. "

Alonzo

Questions:

1. Why do you think Ms. Wells thinks it is important for Alonzo to have people to give him extra hugs and love while his dad is in prison?
2. Why do you think Alonzo was worried his dad would be mad at him?
3. Who do you have that can be there for you during hard times?

Additional Discussion Questions

» How did your friends react when they found out your parent went to jail?
» Is it OK in your family to talk about your parent being in jail?
» Name one person you can talk to about how you feel.
» Who was the first person you told about your parent being in jail?
» Who can you talk to when you're feeling sad?
» Name two people you trust.
» Do you have any friends with a parent in jail?

Activities

{How Much Can You Handle Alone}

Objective: To encourage the child(ren) to utilize support and/or to ask for help

Give the child a balloon and ask him/her to keep it in the air without it touching the ground. After a few seconds, give him/her a second balloon and then a third. Once the child cannot keep the balloons up in the air alone, suggest s/he thinks of some way s/he could possibly keep them up. The child should realize s/he needs to ask you to help him/her. If s/he does not come up with this on his/her own, suggest it to him/her.

For group activity, start out giving one child a balloon and add more until s/he has to ask another group member for help. Try to keep adding balloons until s/he needs to ask more and more group members for help.

Follow-up: Ask the child(ren) to identify times s/he s asked for help in the past or may need to ask for help in the future. Discuss why asking for help is both courageous and smart.

{Tree of Support}

Objective: To identify support systems

Cut out the shape of a tree trunk from a brown piece of paper. Tape the tree trunk to the wall or lay flat on the floor or a large surface. The bigger the better, so the child can visualize having a BIG support system. Provide the child with plenty of paper leaves and have him/her write the names of people who can help support him/her on the leaves. If the child has difficulty thinking of many people, help him/her brainstorm about who s/he knows from school (teachers, kids, office staff, principal, counselor, janitor, etc.), church, family friends, neighborhood, extended family, after school activities, community, etc. Put the leaves on the tree.

For group activity, have each child make his/her own tree. Suggest the children help each other think of people that can support them. Suggest the children ask each other to be part of their support systems.

Follow-up: Ask the child(ren) if s/he is surprised to see so many leaves. Ask child(ren) to identify other feelings associated with seeing this support system.

{Mine Field}

Objective: To help the child(ren) develop trust

Place various small objects on the ground in an indoor or outdoor place. Have the child put on a blind fold and explain the importance of being able to trust people. Ask her/him to trust you to lead her/him through the "mine field" (walking from one end of the space to the other without stepping on an object). Explain that you will do your best to keep him/her safe. Later allow the child to then lead you through the mine field.

For group activity, have the children partner up and blindfold one child in each set. Explain to the seeing child that it is important s/he is trustworthy and that s/he will try her/his best to keep her/his partner safe from stepping on an object. Have the seeing child lead the blindfolded child from one end of the designated area to the other end. After several minutes, have the kids switch roles so the other child is blindfolded instead. Repeat the exercise.

Follow-up: Discuss what s/he liked and didn't like about the trust walk. Why is it hard to keep walking when you are not sure what you will run into? How did it help to have someone there with you that could see? What would have happened if you were alone and couldn't see? When you were the leader, how did you feel about your job? What would have happened if you weren't there for that person?

{Support Needed}

Objective: To identify the need for support systems

Direct the child to make a list of concrete things that need supports, such as bridges, chairs, buildings, tree branches, etc. Ask the child to select one of these objects and to draw a picture of what it would look like with*out* any support.

For group activity, allow the children to work together to come up with the list. Lead the group in the discussion and then have each person chose one thing to draw a picture of.

Follow-up: Ask the child(ren) to share her/his picture. Discuss what would happen if other objects did not have any support. Then discuss what happens to people when they do not have support.

{Asking for Help Role Plays}

Objective: To practice asking for help

Have the child act out the following scenarios and identify who s/he would ask for help in each situation.

For group activity, have the children take turns acting out the scenarios as the one who asks for help and the one being asked for help.

Scenario 1: Micha does not understand how to do his math work. He is still working on it, while most of the other kids are finished.

Scenario 2: Nikya is playing outside by herself and she fell down and hurt herself. She is having problems walking home. She looks around and sees some older boys playing and her neighbor sitting on her porch.

Scenario 3: Mario is feeling angry at his mom for leaving him with his grandma and wants to punch a hole in the wall.

Scenario 4: Paris wants to go to the Mom and Me breakfast at school, but her mom is in jail.

Follow-up: Ask the child(ren) to identify what was easy and/or difficult about asking for help. Discuss why it is important to be able to ask for help. Discuss how s/he feels when others ask *her/him* for help.

Reproducible Worksheets

Reproducible Worksheet 2.1, *Trust*, encourages children to name different people in their lives who they can trust in different ways. If children of incarcerated parents have been disappointed by significant people in their lives and have generalized this experience to others, they may have difficulty trusting, which can hinder hope. It is important to assist them in seeing there *may be* people in their lives who they can count on for specific (vs. global) needs.

Reproducible Worksheet 2.2, *Trust Factors*, lists several features of trust for children to consider in making a decision as to whether or not they should discuss their parent's incarceration with someone. In order to trust someone with this information, children have to assess the integrity and values of the other person. They must evaluate which factors are important and very important to them.

Reproducible Worksheet 2.3, *Appreciating My Caregiver*, asks children to draw a picture of their current caregiver at the beginning of a maze and a picture of themselves at the end of the maze. The maze has places along the way for children are to write down things they appreciate about their caregiver. Many children of incarcerated parents are turned over to extended family members or are placed in foster care. Helping children adjust to new living environments is helpful for other kinds of adjustment (e.g., schools, neighborhoods, etc.).

Reproducible Worksheet 2.4, *Asking for Support*, illustrates effective and ineffective ways to ask for support. Because children are children (and children of incarcerated parents may not have had optimal environments for social/emotional development), guidance is needed in order to teach them how to *ask* for assistance rather than ignore their needs or act out behaviorally.

Reproducible Worksheet 2.5, *Getting Support*, is a word puzzle that, when solved, spells "reach out," an important message for getting support. This is a reinforcing message children of incarcerated parents may need to be proactive in getting the supports they need.

Reproducible Worksheet 2.6, *Helping Hands*, directs children to make multiple copies of a picture of a hand (provided) and to write the names of helpful and available individuals on each one. Children are then directed to post these "helping hands" in a place where they will easily be reminders of people who are supportive. If children have limited support systems, it may be necessary to seek out additional persons who can act as friends, mentors, and surrogate extended family for these children.

Trust

Trust is being able to count on someone. It is believing in and having confidence in that person. But there are different kinds of trust. It is not all or nothing. You may trust one person to laugh at your jokes, but not trust them to keep your secrets. You may trust another person to buy you a holiday gift, but not trust them to remember your birthday. It helps to know what people you can trust and depend on for different needs. Write the names of the people in your life who you can trust for the following things:

1. Someone I trust to always listen to me _____

2. Someone I trust to help me with school work _____

3. Someone I trust to keep me safe from harm _____

4. Someone I trust to cheer me up _____

5. Someone I trust to feed me _____

6. Someone I trust to remember my birthday _____

7. Someone I trust to keep a secret_____

8. Someone I trust to take care of me when I am sick _____

9. Someone I trust to not say mean things to me even if s/he is angry with me _____

10. Someone I trust to be honest with me _____

Trust Factors

You may or may not want to tell other kids your parent is incarcerated. If you do tell someone, it is important to consider who you trust. The kids who you select to tell will need to have certain qualities or trust factors – things *you* think are important. Look at the trust factors listed below. Circle the ones you think a person should have if you decide to tell her/him. Then color red the two which you think are the *most* important.

Would not look shocked when I told her/him

Would not tell other kids about my parent

Would not tell her/his parent about my parent

Would not use the information against me if s/he got mad at me for some reason

Would have things in her/his life that are private, too

Would not think bad of me because of my parent

Would let me talk about it as much as I wanted without changing the subject

Would have something to say to make me feel better

Appreciating My Caregiver

Who is the adult(s) you are currently living with? _____

On the maze below, draw a picture of your caregiver(s) at the start and a picture of you at the end. Go through the maze to connect your caregiver(s) to you. Each time you reach a square with a heart in it, write down one of the things you appreciate about your caregiver.

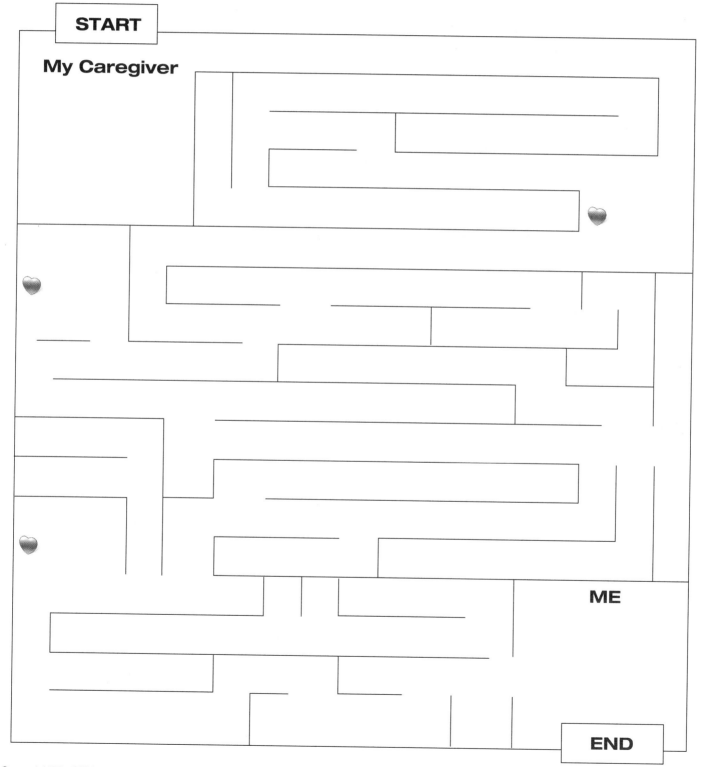

Asking for Support

People don't always know when you need support. After all, they can't read your mind! You often have to ask for support when you need it. In each pair of speech bubbles, there is a good way to ask for support and a bad way to ask for support. Color in the good one.

1

When you have some time, could I talk to you about some things that are bugging me?

What's up?

2

You had better spend more time with me or I'm going to get in a lot more trouble!

I've been feeling pretty lonely lately. Would you mind spending more time with me?

3

<sigh....>

I would love it if we could do something sometime – just the two of us.

4

I'm doing terrible in math. Could you help me after school today?

If I had a better math teacher, I could probably make better grades in math.

Getting Support

Humans are social creatures. We all need support. How do you get support from others? Follow the directions below. Then use the leftover letters to find the answer.

1. Cross off all the P's and Q's

2. Cross off all the vowels in Column 4

3. Cross off all the letters in Row C that come *after* R in the alphabet

4. Cross off all the letters in Column 5 that come *before* F in the alphabet

5. Cross off all the consonants in Row G

6. Cross off all the D's and B's

7. Cross off all the letters in Column 2 that come *after* L in the alphabet

	1	2	3	4	5	6
A	R	M	P	A	Q	B
B	B	E	Q	O	E	P
C	S	D	A	P	A	V
D	Q	Z	P	C	D	B
E	B	N	Q	D	H	Q
F	Q	P	D	O	B	O
G	X	Z	W	P	U	T
H	P	S	B	T	Q	D

___ ___ ___ ___ ___   ___ ___ ___ !!

Helping Hands

Make several copies of the hand below. Then cut them out. On each one write the name of someone who you could ask to help you if you needed something. Place these on your wall or mirror at home to remind yourself to reach out!

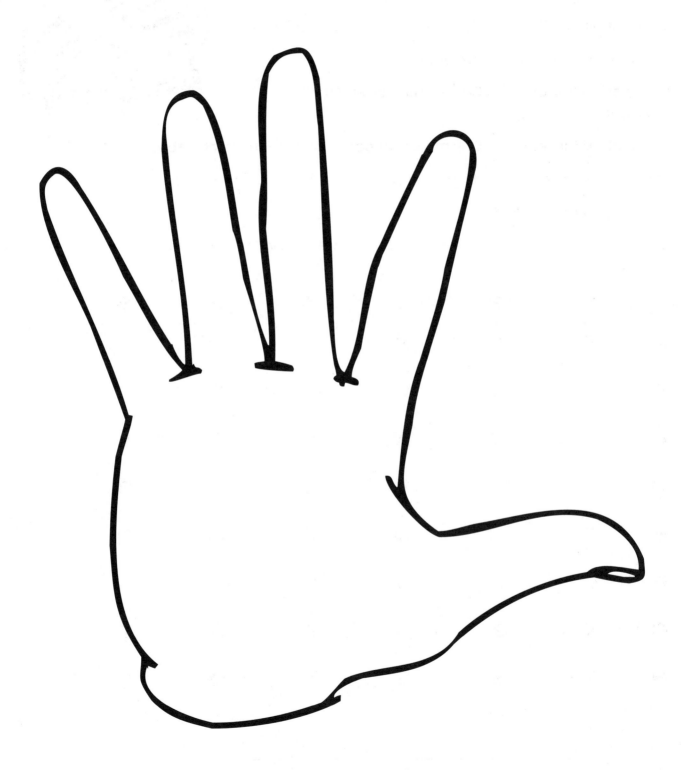

Lesson 3
Dealing with Shame

Notes to Facilitator

Much of the literature regarding children of incarcerated parents identifies social stigma/shame as a major issue needing intervention (e.g., Gabel, 1992). Children are very conscious of the social stigma that comes with having a parent in jail or prison. This stigma can come from a variety of sources including peers, other family members, church members, and community members. While some have held the idea that certain groups consider having a parent in prison normal or a status symbol, Hairston (2002) found this to be a myth. Another study found that in the school environment, students with incarcerated parents were more frequently teased than other students (Jose-Kampfner, 1991). Children of incarcerated parents absolutely experience explicit and subtle discrimination and feel social stigma and shame.

Different from guilt, shame permeates one's self-concept. Whereas guilt says, "You *did* something rotten," shame says, "You *are* rotten." Guilt helps to change negative behavior to positive behavior. Shame only causes humiliation, withdrawal, powerlessness and anger. Children of incarcerated parents often blame themselves and feel overwhelming shame. They believe if they had been good enough, the crimes would not have happened. They think if they were worthy, their parent would be different. These are only two of the cognitive distortions children of incarcerated parents often believe about themselves.

Francine Lucas Sinclair (daughter of Frank Lucas, notorious drug kingpin played by Denzel Washington in the film, *American Gangster*) looked back at her childhood as a child of incarcerated parents and described how she kept the secret of her parents imprisonment for over 20 years due to shame (http://www.blackvoices.com/blogs/2007/12/10/francine-lucas-sinclair-daughter-of-american-gangster/2). The feelings of shame associated with stigma may vary depending on the developmental stage of the child, but some of the effects from stigma and shame can include:

> **Children of incarcerated parents often blame themselves and feel overwhelming shame.**

» Being excluded from social activities

» Being teased or bullied

» Not feeling a sense of belonging

» Having low self-esteem

» Not feeling able to talk about the incarcerated parent or current living conditions

According to cognitive-behavioral theory, unhealthy feelings, such as shame, can be changed by identifying, challenging, and changing the cognitive distortions (or "stinkin' thinkin'") that trigger those feelings. Counselors can assist children of incarcerated parents by helping them "examine the evidence" regarding their cognitive distortions in order to realize they may be personalizing, awfulizing, jumping to conclusions, or practicing emotional reasoning.

Suggestions:

» Reiterate over and over again to children that it is not their fault their parent is incarcerated. Encourage caregivers to do the same.

» Help children identify, challenge and change their cognitive distortions or "stinkin' thinkin.'"

» Create a sense of mutuality and care. A positive relationship with a counselor can become a new template for future relationships without the effects of shame.

» In order to counteract the "shrinking away" effects of shame, assist children in finding healthy ways to "stand out" – e.g., music and drama performances, sports events, art contests, spelling bees, chess clubs, Scouts, etc.

» Assess children's status on the playground and make sure they are not victims of overt or covert bullying. If they are experiencing harassment or rejection, insist the school enforce an anti-bullying program.

» Encourage children to have good posture and to look people in the eye. There is growing evidence of a mind-body connection. If children carry their bodies in strong assertive ways, the mind will interpret this as esteem.

Script

Shame is a feeling people get about themselves when they do not think they are a good person and feel like they are an embarrassment. Sometimes when kids have a parent in jail or prison, they get teased by other kids. They might feel embarrassed about what happened to their family and start to feel shame. Shame is a feeling that is not helpful and needs to be changed. When a kid has a parent go to jail, it does not make the kid a bad person. There is nothing you could have done to keep your parent from going to jail, and what happened is not your fault. Getting rid of bad thinking and using positive thinking is one way to get rid of shame.

Prison Letters

"Dear Dad,

Hi Dad. I wanted to tell you I am not going to let anyone say anything bad about you. A couple of days ago, Billy called you a criminal. Well, I put him in his place and he won't be saying anything else, if you know what I mean. I told all the other kids it was a lie because I felt embarrassed. I don't think it's any of their business anyway. Sometimes I just wish my family was as good as everyone else's. I wish I were as good as the other kids. Well, I gotta go help Grandma with the dishes. I hope you are being good.

I love you,
Alonzo

Dear Alonzo,

First of all, I don't ever want to hear about you hurting another kid again. I also do not want you to use me as an excuse to act out. I feel bad about what I did Son, but I am not ashamed of who I am. I love your mom and my children. I have worked hard for them and tried to care for them the best I could at the time. Yes, you have a parent with problems, but who doesn't? Everyone goes through hard times. I am proud of my kids. My kids are my greatest accomplishments. I wake up every day feeling proud of you and the good things you have been doing. You are a good kid. You work hard at your grades, you are kind to others, and you are a great son and brother. I understand you feel embarrassed, but I want to make sure you know you have not done anything wrong. I feel embarrassed about what I did too, but we will get through this.

Remember I am proud of you."

Love, Dad

Questions:

1. What could Alonzo have done differently when Billy called his dad a criminal?

2. Is there a difference between feeling embarrassed and feeling ashamed?

3. If you were Alonzo, how would you feel?

Additional Discussion Questions

» Have you ever felt like you shouldn't be sad that your parent is in jail?

» Do you think it is your fault your parent is in jail?

» Is anything better with your parent in jail?

» What do you tell other people when they ask about your parent?

» Has anyone teased you because you have a parent in jail?

» Do you feel like you have to keep it a secret that your parent is in jail?

Activities

{Ice Cube}

Objective: To understand the benefits of sharing feelings instead of keeping them inside

Give the child an ice cube to hold in his/her hand. Explain as long as ice cubes remain locked alone in the freezer, they will remain hard and cold. As soon as they are out in the open and start to let the outside people see what they are, they will start to melt. Explain to the child that our feelings of shame, guilt, and sadness are like the ice cubes. Sometimes we keep these feelings hidden inside because we don't want others to see them, but when we start to share these feelings with friends or people we trust, it is like we take our feelings out of the freezer. The warmth of others can help melt the ice and help our feelings start to soften.

For group activity, give each child his/her own ice cube. Allow children to share with the group if they can think of any ways their feelings have been like ice cubes.

Follow-up: Give child(ren) the opportunity to discuss any feelings s/he has been having related having an incarcerated parent. Help the child(ren) identify any feelings of relief, comfort, calm, support, etc. that s/he feels sharing this information.

{Chasing Away Shame}

Objective: To externalize feelings of shame

Explain to the child that shame is when a person feels bad about her/himself and thinks s/he is not a valuable person. Ask the child draw a picture of her/him chasing shame away. In the picture, s/he should give shame a message, like "You are a Liar," "Get Away From Me," "Be Quiet," etc.

For group activity, have each child draw his/her own picture. Give the children the opportunity to share their pictures with the group.

Follow-up: Give the child(ren) the opportunity to discuss feelings of shame s/he has experienced and how s/he makes them go away.

{Stop the Stinkin' Thinkin' Game}

Objective: To help child(ren) replace untrue/unhelpful thoughts with thoughts that are more realistic and helpful

Cut out examples of untrue or unhelpful thoughts in Appendix B. Have the child read the thoughts out loud one at a time. Ask the child if this thought is a helpful thought. When s/he says no, tell her/him you are going to help him/her stop thinking that thought. When the child reads the thought out loud a second time, yell **STOP!** in the middle of the thought. Ask the child to then identify a more positive or helpful thought. For example, the unhelpful thought might be, "I'm stupid." The child could then say, "Even though I don't understand some things, I am smart in other things."

*For group activity, the children take turns reading the thoughts out loud one at a time. Ask the group if this thought was a helpful thought. When they say no, tell them to help the child stop thinking that thought. When the child reads the thought out loud a second time, have the group yell **STOP!** in the middle of the thought. Ask the child to tell the group something s/he would rather think about.*

Follow-up: Give the child(ren) the opportunity to discuss any untrue or unhelpful thoughts s/he has had about her/himself or their parent in prison. Assist her/him in coming up with more positive, realistic and helpful thoughts.

{The Weight of Shame}

Objective: To identify the negative effects of holding onto shame

Fill a backpack with heavy books or bricks. Have a child wear the backpack and walk around the room for a few minutes. When it becomes clear the child has felt the weight of the backpack, have them stop. Explain the backpack was full of shame, and it is time to get rid of the shame. Take the items out of the backpack while stating reasons the child does not need to feel ashamed. For example, "You don't need to feel ashamed because what happened is not your fault."

After all the shame has been taken out of the backpack, have the child wear it and walk around the room again.

For group activity, have the children take turns wearing the filled backpack before taking the shame out of it, and then let them take turns again wearing the empty backpack. Lead the group in a discussion about the activity.

Follow-up: Discuss how it was different carrying the backpack with and without the shame. Ask the child(ren) how it might feel to be without the shame in her/his day to day life(s).

{Helpful or Unhelpful}

Objective: To connect unhelpful thoughts to feelings of shame.

Read the following thoughts out loud and ask the child to determine if it is a helpful thought or an unhelpful thought. Explain that focusing on unhelpful thoughts can make it harder to get rid of shame. For each unhelpful thought, ask the child to identify a helpful thought to replace it with.

For group activity the children can take turns identifying if the thoughts are helpful or not and replacing the unhelpful thoughts with helpful ones.

Thoughts:
» My mom or dad will never come home.
» Things will be ok.
» Everyone thinks I am weird because my parent is in jail.
» It is good to feel happy about my life.
» I will end up just like my parent who is in jail.
» No one will like me if they find out about my family.
» I can get good grades in school and feel proud of myself.
» It was my fault my parent had to leave.
» I am a good person.
» People care about me.

Follow-up: Ask the child(ren) to identify specific feelings (i.e. happy, content, sad, angry, scared, worried, ashamed, etc.) associated with the different kinds of thinking.

Reproducible Worksheets

Reproducible Worksheet 3.1, *Looking at Shame,* lists various dimensions of shame and asks children to check and rank those which apply to them. Children may not recognize the subtle ways in which shame causes them to feel inadequate, angry or apologetic. Helping them to label the specific ways in which shame plays out in their lives can assist them in resisting shame's power.

Reproducible Worksheet 3.2, *Looking at Stigma,* defines stigma as "feeling like <you have> a bad reputation for no fault of your own." It points out that stigma can come from peers, family members, people at church, people in the community, etc., but suggests coping skills can be used for some of the effects of stigma. Stigma for children of incarcerated parents can be reduced in their communities through education and awareness campaigns, but children will benefit from using coping skills for those times when others have been less than sensitive.

Reproducible Worksheet 3.3, *Get Rid of that Stinkin' Thinkin',* explains that feelings of shame can come from negative thinking - or "stinkin' thinkin." Children are introduced to the cognitive distortions of personalization, emotional reasoning and jumping to conclusions. They are then asked to read examples of "stinkin' thinkin'" that might be used by children of incarcerated parents and identify the type of cognitive distortion it represents. Identifying cognitive distortions is an important step to changing them. Indeed, since cognitive restructuring has been shown to be effective with many internalizing disorders (Grossman, & Hughes, 1992), facilitators should regularly assist children in identifying, challenging and changing their "stinkin' thinkin."

Reproducible Worksheet 3.4, *Fishing for Positive Self-talk,* asks children to find positive self-statements and mark out the negative self-statements. Numerous studies have shown that self-talk greatly influences mood and affect. It is important for children of incarcerated parents to practice eliminating negative self-talk by using affirming self-talk.

Reproducible Worksheet 3.5, *Standing Out,* asks children to fight off shame's message to shrink back by doing just the opposite – stand out. Several constructive ways to stand out are listed, and children are asked to circle the ways they would like to stand out. Shame says, "There's something wrong with me, so I need to hide." Helping children to find ways to feel proud can ameliorate shame's effects.

Looking at Shame

Shame is a feeling of embarrassment or disgrace. It creates deep fear that is very painful; it tricks people into believing they are bad. Sometimes children who have parents in jail or prison feel shame. Look at some of the features of shame below and check the ones you experience. For each one you have checked, go back and rate how much of a problem this is for you (1 = a little bit and 5 = a lot!). Then answer the question at the bottom of the page.

	if yes ✔	If yes, circle the level in which you feel it				
I feel ugly, flawed or damaged		1	2	3	4	5
I have a hard time trusting others		1	2	3	4	5
I feel like others judge me		1	2	3	4	5
I feel like I have to apologize a lot		1	2	3	4	5
When I argue, I feel like I have to fight		1	2	3	4	5
I feel less than other kids		1	2	3	4	5
I feel like others are against me		1	2	3	4	5
I get very angry when others criticize me		1	2	3	4	5
I worry that other parents will not allow their children to play with me		1	2	3	4	5
I am afraid that others will discover my secrets		1	2	3	4	5

Just because your parent is in jail or prison does not mean that s/he is a bad person. Good people can do bad things. What can you tell yourself in order to let go of shame?

_____

_____

Looking at Stigma

Sometimes when children have a parent in jail or prison, they experience stigma. Stigma is a feeling of disgrace or embarrassment around other people; it can feel like having a bad reputation for no fault of your own. Stigma can come from peers, family members, people at church, or people in the community. Listed below on the left are some of the effects of stigma. Listed below on the right are some coping skills to fight stigma. Circle any of the effects of stigma you are experiencing and then draw lines from those effects to those coping skills you think would help you.

EFFECTS OF STIGMA

Having feelings of depression

Keeping parent's whereabouts a secret

Staying away from others

Bullying or teasing from others

Being talked about or gossiped about by others

Getting left out of things

COPING SKILLS

Talk to a grown-up about the situation and my feelings

Tell myself that it's not my fault and that I am a good person

Stick up for myself using my words

Do something fun with people who care about me

Write a letter to my parent

Get Rid of that Stinkin' Thinkin'

Feelings of shame can come from negative thinking - or "stinkin' thinkin'." Three kinds of "stinkin' thinkin'" are:

- **Personalization:** believing you are responsible for something you are really not responsible for ("If I would have been a better kid, my parent would not have felt he had to go out and get in trouble.")

- **Emotional reasoning:** assuming that feelings are reality ("I feel ashamed of what my parent did, so I am shameful.")

- **Jumping to conclusions:** thinking negatively without the facts ("My parent is in jail, so I will probably go to jail.")

Look at the statements below and circle the kind of "stinkin' thinkin'" it represents. Then answer the questions.

1. "No one is going to want to be my friend if they find out about my parent."

   Personalization   Emotional reasoning   Jumping to conclusions

2. "It's my fault our family has so many problems."

   Personalization   Emotional reasoning   Jumping to conclusions

3. "I'm embarrassed, so I shouldn't talk about it."

   Personalization   Emotional reasoning   Jumping to conclusions

4. "No one probably wants to play with me."

   Personalization   Emotional reasoning   Jumping to conclusions

Which kind of "stinkin' thinkin'" do you use?

_____

_____

What can you tell yourself to make yourself feel better?

_____

_____

Fishing for Positive Self-talk

Feelings of stigma and shame can be fought off with realistic, positive thinking. Look at the self-statements on the fish below. Cross off the fish with negative statements (that might cause you to feel shameful or worthless). Draw a line to the fishing pole from the fish with positive statements (that would cause you to feel confident and satisfied).

"I'm stupid."

"I'm OK."

"I stink."

"I'm a valuable person."

"No one likes me."

"I'm likeable."

"I can do lots of things."

Standing Out

Shame can make you feel like shrinking back, so a good way to fight off shame is by *standing out*. Listed below are some positive ways to *stand out*. Circle the ways you would like to stand out.

Have perfect attendance at school

Open a door for someone

Dress nicely

Score points in a game

Enter a contest

Save my money to buy something special

Give someone a compliment

Send a thank you card

Send a sympathy card

Tell a joke

Plan a party

Enter a project in the science fair

Stand up for someone

Earn a badge in scouts

Perform in a play

Perform in a concert

Make a 100% on my school work

Fix my hair in a different style

Do someone a favor

Keep the neatest desk

Smile at everyone

Answer with "Ma'am" or "Sir" to the teacher

Lesson 4
Allowing for Grief

Notes to Facilitator

Children of incarcerated parents face disenfranchised grief. Disenfranchised grief is experienced when a person's pain is not validated by society. Individuals with disenfranchised grief do not feel they can publicly acknowledge or openly mourn their loss. Their bereavement becomes more difficult and prolonged as a result (Beck & Jones, 2007). This is experienced in many ways by children of incarcerated parents because they are unable to share their sadness with peers or adults who may themselves feel the parent deserves to be in jail and the child should be glad the parent is gone.

While a loss from death is final, the loss from incarceration is ambiguous; children may be confused about how to grieve the loss of a parent who is alive but emotionally and physically absent (Miller, 2006). This can be extremely confusing for children. With nonfinite loss, pain is continuous. Family members are denied the hope and expectations they had for the person who in incarcerated (Jones & Beck, 2007). Children of incarcerated parents experience this type of grief in a number of ways. Parental rights might be terminated by the court following a parent's arrest, and a child might have to grieve this loss. Even when parental rights remain intact, the parent misses significant milestones in a child's life. A child grieves that unmet expectation. When experiencing disenfranchised grief and nonfinite loss, grieving is extremely confusing for children. They may numb and "stuff" their feelings or they may experience ambivalent and conflicting feelings (i.e., relief and worry; love and anger).

In most cases (but not all), a continued relationship between a child and an incarcerated parent is important for the child's development. However, there are multiple factors that disrupt this bond from being fostered. The majority of prisoners are held in facilities located more than 100 miles from their homes (Mumola, 2000). Geographic distance and visitation procedures are often uncomfortable or humiliating and can make visiting imprisoned family members difficult. It is not surprising, then, that more than half of parents in prison never receive a personal visit (Mumola, 2000). Another hurdle can be found in attempting telephone contact because of the expense of collect calling where additional fees are placed on calls made from a prison (Travis, 2005). The financial burden of driving long distances and paying for expensive telephone calls makes it difficult to maintain a relationship with a parent who is incarcerated, especially for families already stretched monetarily from taking in the parent's child(ren).

> **When experiencing disenfranchised grief and nonfinite loss, grieving is extremely confusing for children.**

There is a body of best practices for children's grief due to loss from death. These guidelines include giving children information about the loss as well as fostering open conversations about the grieving process. It is well-recognized that grieving children may need assistance in their expression of emotions attached to grief (Kaufman & Kaufman, 2005). Indeed, negative outcomes have been found in children whose parents avoided the topic of loss, did not involve the children in the grieving process, and did not validate the child's grief (Kaufman & Kaufman, 2005). These principles directly apply to children whose parents are incarcerated because they are often shielded from the negative aspects of a parent's incarceration due to social stigma and family members' unwillingness to involve them in adult matters (Travis, 2005). Though adults withhold basic information to protect children, withholding may actually heighten children's feelings of stress and uncertainty.

Suggestions:

» Allow children to express any and all feelings surrounding grief and loss. Let them know grief is normal and they are not crazy or pathological if they feel sad or angry or worried. Assure children the incarceration is not their fault – even if they had wished it prior to the arrest.

» Grief often causes people to look for someone to blame. Children may blame themselves or the police or other people involved in the illegal activity. If children are blaming others, simply offer up the idea that grief often causes us to look for blame.

» Do not compare losses. Each child's experience of loss is felt at a 100% for them.

» Find healthy ways to talk about the incarcerated parent (e.g., stories, photos, etc.). Encourage children to speak frequently about him/her.

» Facilitate/encourage visitation and phone communication. Provide transportation or assist caregivers in obtaining additional funds to pay for these contacts. There are programs and grants available to support parent-child bonds in prison. Research these in your area.

Script

Kids feel grief when their parent goes to jail. Grief is a mix of feelings people have when they have lost something important to them. It is made up of feelings of sadness, anger, loneliness and worry all felt at once. It is very normal to have grief when you go through a difficult time. It is hard for kids not to be able to see or talk to their parent like they used to. There are ways to feel better. Talking about your parent who is in jail or prison can help. It is good to talk about your memories of your parent, whether they are good or bad. And it is OK to think about your parent. If possible, write your parent letters and visit him/her. Just remember it is OK and normal to feel sad, angry, lonely, and worried, AND it is also OK to feel happy.

Prison Letters

"Dear Alonzo,

Hi, Son. I don't have much time to write. I just wanted to tell you some good news. I just got a job here. I get to work in the kitchen and help make the meals. I am really looking forward to having something to do. Every week I can spend some of the money I make in the store here and get some comfortable shoes, clothes, snacks, and stuff like that. The hardest part of being here is how much I miss you and your brothers and sister. I keep remembering all the funny times we had like that time I slipped on the wet floor in the grocery store and pulled you down with me. We laughed so hard I almost wet my pants. That was a good time. By the way, I never answered your questions from your first letter. There are fights here, but I try and stay away from them. As for your question about me digging a tunnel - well, I think that only happens in the movies.

Love, Dad

Dear Dad,

I feel bad I haven't been writing you as many letters. I don't really know what to tell you about. I don't want to tell you the things that are going wrong because I don't want you to worry like I am. The truth is I miss you a lot. Sometimes I cry because I miss you so much. It was hard at school this week during parent night. Some of my old teachers asked where you were. At first I was sad, but then I just got angry and wouldn't talk to anybody. Everyone keeps telling me it is ok to feel upset, and it will help to think about the good times we had together. Grandma bought me a picture frame to put a picture of you in to look at when I miss you the most. It made me laugh that you thought about falling down at the grocery store. I didn't even think you would remember that. It seems like it helps you to think about the good times too. You are a good dad.

I love you Dad."

Alonzo

Questions:

1. Why do you think people tell Alonzo it is OK to feel sad?
2. How do you think looking at a picture of his dad might help Alonzo?
3. What else can Alonzo do to feel better?

Additional Discussion Questions

» What is something in your life your parent has missed because of being in jail?

» Is it hard to tell your parent something bad that happened to you?

» How did you feel when your parent went to jail?

» Do you have a favorite memory of your parent before s/he went to jail?

» Do you ever feel guilty about having fun while your parent is in jail?

» What is something you want your parent to know right now?

» Can you write or call your parent? Which do you like to do?

» What do you do when you need to talk to your parent but can't?

Activities

{Feelings Charades}

Objective: To increase the feelings vocabulary of the child(ren) and make her/him more comfortable talking about feelings

Write feelings words associated with grief on pieces of paper (i.e. sad, worried, embarrassed, lonely, confused, scared, angry, etc.), fold them and mix them up. Take turns with the child selecting a feeling (so that the other does not see it) and then acting it out. After guessing correctly, say things like "I could tell you were sad because you were looking down and the floor and pretending to cry" or "You were angry because your muscles were tight, your face was scrunched up, and your hands were fists." Let the child also describe with words how s/he knew what feeling to guess.

For group activity, have the children take turns acting out the feelings and guessing.

Follow-up: Ask the child(ren) to tell about a time s/he felt these various feelings.

{My Feelings First Aid Kit}

Objective: To provide the child(ren) with coping skills for negative feelings

Provide child with a small box, bag, or some type of container s/he can decorate. Give her/him a copy of Appendix C, and allow her/him to cut out the pictures of the different medical supplies. Tell the child when s/he feels very sad, scared, mad, or worried, s/he can tell her/himself things or do things to feel better. Tell the child to write down some things s/he can say or do to feel better on the different pictures. The child should put the pictures in her/his kit. Tell the child to pull a paper out of the survival kit when s/he is feeling upset and needs something to help her/him feel better.

For group activity, allow each child to make his/her own first aid kit. Have the kids help each other come up with ideas of things they can do to feel better.

Follow-up: Give the child(ren) opportunities to discuss times s/he felt very sad, scared, mad, or worried, and what s/he could do to make her/himself feel better if s/he experiences those feelings again.

{The Person I Miss}

Objective: To help the child(ren) grieve the loss of their incarcerated parent

Give the child the list of descriptive words in Appendix D. There are blank spots for you and the child to add more if you like. Have the child paste a photo or draw a picture of his/her incarcerated parent in the middle of a large piece of paper. Have the child choose as many words as s/he wants that remind him/her of the parent and write the words around the picture. You may modify this exercise by cutting out the descriptive words and gluing them around the picture.

For group activity, allow each child to do his/her own project. Give children the opportunity to share their pictures with each other and to tell about their incarcerated parents.

Follow-up: Give the child(ren) an opportunity to talk about her/his incarcerated parent and what s/he misses about her/him.

{Photo Frame}

Objective: To give the child(ren) a visual connection to their incarcerated parent

Make photo frames out of popsicle sticks. Decorate the frame (after it has been put together) with glitter, food colored rice, foam cutouts, or whatever you have available. Glue a piece of yarn to the top two corners of the frame so it can be hung up on a tack or nail on the child's wall. Allow the child to bring a picture of his/her incarcerated parent to tape in the frame (or s/he can take the frame home and get a picture there). If the child does not have a picture of the parent, some Department of Corrections websites have pictures of inmates that can be printed out. This could be done by the facilitator prior to the group or the child could do it her/himself (depending on child ability and computer access).

For group activity, allow each child to make his/her own picture frame and share the pictures with the group.

Follow-up: Ask the child(ren) where they are going to keep their picture, and when s/he will look at it. Ask the child(ren) if this is how s/he remembers the parent.

{Memory Book}

Objective: To focus on positive memories about the incarcerated parent

Ask the child to come up with several happy memories about his/her incarcerated parent. This may be very different for each child depending on whether or not s/he lived with the parent, how long the parent has been incarcerated, etc. Have the child create a memory book in which s/he writes or draws pictures of these different positive memories. If the child needs help coming up with memories, you may suggest s/he comes up with a holiday memory, a birthday memory, something fun they did together, a time they laughed, a time their parent said something important to him/her, etc.

For group activity, have each child make his/her own memory book.

Follow-up: Give the child(ren) the opportunity to vocalize what s/he misses about his/her parent in prison. Remind the child that no one can ever take away the memories that s/he has.

{Chinese Proverb}

Objective: To identify the benefits of not dwelling on negative feelings

Ask the child to think about the Chinese proverb, "You cannot prevent the birds of sorrow from flying over your head, but you can prevent them from building nests in your hair." Discuss what this means to the child.

For group activity, have each child describe how s/he would keep the "birds of sorrow" from "building nests in your hair." Children can draw pictures of this.

Follow-up: Ask the child(ren) if s/he has been dwelling on any negative thoughts. Discuss ways in which s/he can keep these thoughts from staying in her/his mind too long.

Reproducible Worksheets

Reproducible Worksheet 4.1, *Complete These Sentences …,* asks children to remember their parent. It addresses memories and wishes. Grief literature stresses how important it is to talk about memories of the missing person. In fact, 30-90% of the pages in children's grief workbooks are dedicated to memories of the lost loved one.

Reproducible Worksheet 4.2, *Feelings,* directs children to identify various feelings and then to rewrite the word, "Grief" using letters from the other feelings. This familiarizes children with feelings words and the grief label. Having a name ("grief") to describe the myriad of feelings children have about their incarcerated parent will help them to better understand and process their grieving.

Reproducible Worksheet 4.3, *Measuring Feelings of Grief,* invites children to measure feeling sad, worried, angry, and lonely on a thermometer. This worksheet can be used as part of an assessment to identify children's perceptions of their most problematic feelings.

Reproducible Worksheet 4.4, *Sad Feelings,* asks children to circle descriptive words associated with their sad feelings. Some of these words include lost, dull, alone, broken-hearted and heavy. It is important to *not* minimize children's sadness and grief – in fact, it is important to facilitate their expressions of sadness and grief. It has been suggested that the more one can mindfully face the pain of grief, the greater possibility of decreasing its effects.

Reproducible Worksheet 4.5, *Worries,* asks children to identify some of their personal worries by circling worries from a list. For children, the loss of a parent represents multiple losses – i.e., the loss of income, the loss of emotional support, the loss of a co-parent for the remaining parent, the loss of a mentor/person to seek advice from, the loss of play time with that parent, etc. These losses create worry for children. Facilitators can use this worksheet to assist children to either identify their cognitive distortions or use problem-solving skills.

Complete These Sentences ...

Read the sentence starters below and then write in the endings.

1. The thing that is hardest for me about having a parent in jail/prison is

_____ .

2. My favorite memory of my parent is

_____ .

3. My worst memory of my parent is

_____ .

4. If I could talk to my parent right now I would ask

_____ .

5. If I could talk to my parent right now I would tell her/him

_____ .

6. When my parent went away to jail/prison, I

_____ .

7. Since my parent went away, I can't

_____ .

8. Since my parent went away, my friends

_____ .

9. Since my parent went away, my family

_____ .

10. When I am alone, I

_____ .

Feelings

DIRECTIONS: Use the words from the Words Box below to complete the sentences. Then write the circled letters in the spaces at the bottom of the page. It spells out a very important feeling that needs to be talked about!

```
                    WORDS BOX
    WORRIED      ANGRY        LONELY
    FEELINGS     CONFUSED     FRIENDS
```

1. When I feel ___ ___ ◯ ___ ___ , I sometimes say and do things I regret.

2. Other words for ___ ___ ___ ◯ ___ ___ ___ are 'concerned,' 'anxious,' and 'nervous.'

3. All of us have lots of different ___ ___ ___ ___ ◯ ___ ___ ___ when we experience troubled times.

4. When I am alone and want to be with someone who is not available, I can feel
___ ___ ___ ◯ ___ ___.

5. I feel ___ ___ ___ ◯ ___ ___ ___ ___ when I don't understand what is happening.

Write down the letters that are circled. The feelings and heartache of losing someone is

called ◯ ◯ ◯ ◯ ◯ .
       1   2   3   4   5

Measuring Feelings of Grief

When we lose or are separated for a long time from someone we love, we grieve. Grieving means feeling the weight of many gloomy feelings. While it is quite normal to grieve a loss, it can help to identify specific feelings that have come with the loss.

Look at the thermometers and feeling words below. Imagining the top of thermometers mean the most and the bottom of the thermometers mean the least, measure each of the feelings by coloring in the two sides of each thermometer – the left side for how you felt when your parent left and the right side for how you feel now.

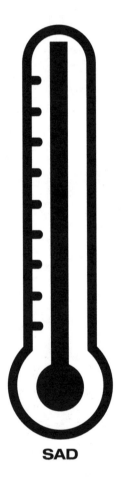 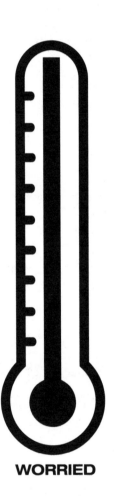 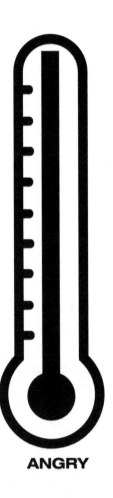 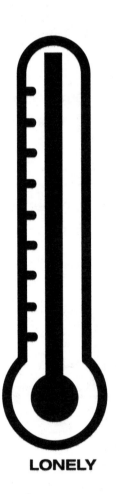

SAD   **WORRIED**   **ANGRY**   **LONELY**

Sad Feelings

Lots of kids who have a parent in jail have sad feelings. Think about your sad feelings. Then look at the words below and color the ones blue that fit your feelings of sadness.

cry

tired

dull

alone

heavy

grumpy

whimper

bored

friendless

sleepy

lost

depressed

dark

negative

broken-hearted

What helps you handle these feelings? _____

_____

Worries

Many kids who have a parent in jail have worries. Not all of them have the same worries, but most of them have some kind of worries. What are *your* worries? Look at the list below and circle the worries you have. Feel free to add any others that are not listed. Then go back and put a '1' by the one you worry about the most often and a '2' by the one you worry about the second most often.

Parent in prison getting sick

Parent in prison getting hurt

Caregiver getting sick

Caregiver being stressed out

Family members using drugs or alcohol

Brothers and sisters not being safe

Brothers and sisters not being together

Brothers' and sisters' feelings

Money problems

Where I am going to live

Getting sick myself

School work

Violence in my neighborhood

Lesson 5
Acknowledging Trauma

Notes to Facilitator

Children of incarcerated parents can experience trauma symptoms such as nightmares, fear of darkness, depression, somatic complaints and fear of isolation (Gabel, 1992; Lowenstein, 1986). Traumatic stress occurs when a child is exposed to a psychological shock and has great difficulty coping with the event. Children who see a parent being arrested experience a trauma similar to seeing their parent assaulted (Mazza, 2002). Children of incarcerated parents may also have experienced other kinds of trauma prior to the arrest. For example, they may have witnessed domestic or community violence, or they may have experienced physical or sexual abuse.

Johnston (1995) found while studying the impacts of parental imprisonment on children, normal development can be affected by the trauma of parental imprisonment. Emotional development is particularly affected by trauma as trauma interferes with the normal developmental processes of learning to control emotions. Behaviors resulting from these out of control emotions include aggression, learning problems, regressed behavior, and acting out. When children have experienced multiple traumas, such as seeing a parent arrested, living in violent or unstable environments, experiencing stigma/shame, symptoms of Posttraumatic Stress Disorder (PTSD) become quite evident (Trzcinski, Satyanathan, & Ferro, 2002). Indeed, the experience of even one trauma impairs children's ability to recover from future traumas. These symptoms often include intrusive thoughts about the trauma, nightmares, avoidance of things that remind them of the event, difficulty sleeping, irritability, and difficulty concentrating (Stein, Jaycox, Kataoka, Rhodes, & Vestal, 2003).

Families with an arrested loved one frequently feel helpless and confused. Children often have unhelpful or untrue cognitions surrounding the traumatic event, such as the belief they did something wrong and caused their parent to leave them (Cunningham, 2001). Research has shown that many cognitive-behavioral interventions can help alleviate the symptoms of trauma-related stress (Stein, et. al., 2003; Cohen, Mannarino, Murray, & Igelman, 2006). Interventions that have been proven to be effective include providing children with psychoeducation about the traumatic event and how our thoughts, feelings, and actions are all related. This helps children understand what and why they are having some of their trauma-related symptoms. Relaxation training, such as controlled breathing and progressive muscle relaxation, helps to combat anxiety (Cohen, Mannarino, Murray, & Igelman, 2006). Cognitive therapy can help to change the maladaptive thoughts children develop surrounding the traumatic event (Cohen, Mannarino, & Deblinger, 2006, p.107).

> **Emotional development is particularly affected by trauma as trauma interferes with the normal developmental processes of learning to control emotions.**

Real life exposure and/or imaginal or creative exposure to fear producing situations are cornerstones of PTSD treatment. These help children decrease the intense anxiety and discomfort that surround memories of the traumatic event. Social problem solving techniques can help children combat the anger and impulsivity that can follow a traumatic event (Jaycox, 2004).

Suggestions:

» Normalize children's reactions to the traumatic event. Let them know it is common for children to have nightmares, have difficulty concentrating, anger, and fear after such an event.

» Teach children relaxation exercises. There are many relaxation strategies including guided imagery, progressive muscle relaxation, meditation, and music.

» Help children to increase their feelings vocabulary by identifying feelings within their bodies. Explain that thoughts, feelings, and actions are all interrelated.

» Engage families in helping to challenge unhelpful or untrue thoughts children may have about their parent's imprisonment.

» Allow children to talk about the trauma over and over again. This is a desensitization technique. Children will have less anxiety surrounding the memories of the event the more they talk about it.

Script

A trauma is an event where a person feels completely helpless or hopeless. Kids who have parents in jail have often experienced trauma. Some kids have seen adults or even their parents hurt each other. Other kids have seen their parents get arrested, which can be a very scary and confusing experience. Other things that can be traumatic for kids are being physically or sexually abused; seeing or hearing about a loved one get hurt; the death or loss of a loved one or witnessing a death; and many other things. When a person goes through trauma, it is normal to feel scared much of the time, to feel angry, to have nightmares, to try and avoid things that remind you of the trauma, to picture what happened over and over again, and to feel shame or guilt about what happened. It is important to realize these feelings are normal. To feel better, talk about what happened with a counselor or trusted adult. Learn ways to help yourself calm down when you feel upset. Get rid of thoughts that are untrue or unhelpful about your trauma and replace them with true thoughts.

Prison Letters

Dear Dad,

How are you? I am writing you this letter for you and Ms. Wells. Ms. Wells told me it would help me to write out my story and that I should tell you some of my feelings. She says this might start to help me stop having nightmares and daydreaming in class. Anyway, I have a problem with thinking about you all the time and about the police coming to our house. I was watching TV in the living room when they just came into our house. They had their guns out and started screaming at me. You and mom and Jenny were still asleep, so when you woke up and started acting like you were going to fight the police, I was scared they were going to shoot you. When you were trying to talk to me and the policeman yelled at you, and then pushed you, I thought it was my fault he pushed you. I am sorry I made him yell at you and hurt you. After they drove away, I thought I would never see you again. I still think sometimes I will never see you again. I also told Ms. Wells I think it is my fault you had to sell drugs because mom said one time you had to do it because she had so many mouths to feed. Maybe if you only had three kids, you would have had enough food without me. Now I have nightmares a lot that the police are taking you away and shooting you. I also think you will get killed in prison. I hope you aren't mad at me for being afraid. I didn't want to tell you this, but Ms. Wells asked me to.

Alonzo

Dear Son,

I cried when I got your letter. The truth is I think about that day all the time too. I keep thinking you should never have had to see that stuff. The look on your face is hard to get out of my head. I am not mad at you for being afraid, but I don't want you to be afraid. I am safe here for the most part. I want you to listen to me – none of this is your fault. If this is anyone's fault, it's mine. I should have been a better father. I should have found another way to make money. I should have finished school. I am sorry Son. I am proud of you. Keep talking to this Ms. Wells. She sounds like a smart lady. I hope you can visit soon. Keep writing.

Love, Dad

Questions:

1. Does anything Alonzo said he is experiencing remind you of what we said about trauma?

2. Do you agree that Alonzo should think what happened is his fault? Why or why not?

3. Why do you think Alonzo's dad cried?

Additional Discussion Questions

» Did you see your parent get arrested?
» Have you ever seen your parent fight where someone got hurt?
» Do you have any nightmares about your parent's arrest? Do you have any nightmares about him/her being in jail? About things that happened before s/he went to jail?
» What was a scary part of your parent going to jail?
» Did you have to move/change schools when your parent went to jail? What was that like?
» Do you ever find it hard to concentrate because you keep thinking about your parent?
» Name two things you don't like about your life since your parent has been in jail.

Activities

{Junk in my Bucket}

Objective: To normalize common reactions to trauma

Crumple up a several pieces of paper. Put a trash can near the child. Remind the child when someone experiences a trauma, there is some common junk that people go through afterwards. Read the list of common reactions to trauma (below) one at a time and tell the child if s/he thinks s/he has experienced this kind of junk, throw a ball of paper in the trash can.

For group activity, have each child throw his/her own piece of paper in the trash can when s/he hears a reaction to trauma s/he has experienced. Be sure to set some ground rules prior to the exercise about making it a safe place for people to share and to not laugh at or disrespect anyone else.

Common Reactions to Trauma

1. Nightmares
2. Thinking about it much of the time
3. Not enjoying things you used to think were fun
4. Feeling sad a lot
5. Having a feeling you will not live a long life
6. Getting startled easily or being jumpy
7. Problems paying attention in school
8. Feeling angry
9. Stomach aches
10. Trouble sleeping
11. Getting nervous a lot
12. Being irritated with others pretty easily
13. Feeling bad about yourself
14. Blaming yourself for what happened
15. Staying away from others or being lonely

Follow-up: Let the child(ren) express how it feels to know these reactions are normal. Discuss which reactions s/he has experienced.

{Belly Breathing Balloons}

Objective: To provide the child(ren) with coping skills to help him/her feel better when upset or anxious

Explain to the child that sometimes when we are upset, we can use belly breathing to help ourselves feel better and feel more relaxed. Belly breathing is when you breathe in slowly and deeply (counting to 5 in your head) as your belly and lungs fill up with air. Watch your belly stick out as you breathe in. Then slowly let the air out and watch your belly go back in as the air is slowly pushed out. Give the child a balloon, blow up the balloons, and allow the child to decorate his/her balloon with magic markers. Have the child lie down and put the balloon on his/her belly. Instruct the child to watch his/her balloon rise up on his/her belly like a hot air balloon as s/he breathes in and land gently as s/he breathes out. Have the child take 5-7 deep belly breaths.

For group activity, have each child blow up and decorate his/her own balloon. Practice doing the belly breaths as a group.

Follow-up: Have the child(ren) identify on a scale of 1-10 how relaxed s/he felt before and after doing the belly breaths. Discuss times of the day (or situations) that s/he could use this technique to stay relaxed and calm.

{Extreme Makeover – Bad Dream Edition}

Objective: To empower the child(ren) to change bad dreams/ nightmares

Direct the child to draw a picture of a bad dream s/he has had. When s/he completes the picture, have the child turn the picture upside down and look it over for the new image that seems to be present in this upside down state (hopefully something completely different or funny). You may need to assist the child in seeing something different. After this discussion, have the child add more marks/coloring to the upside down picture to detail this new version and complete its "make-over."

For group activity, have each child draw his/her own picture. Allow group members to share their pictures with each other and help each other find new funny things in the upside down pictures.

Follow-up: Ask the child(ren) to use her/his imagination to describe a new, entertaining or funny ending to her/his bad dream(s). (Remember that in dreams you can do anything – fly, leap tall buildings, melt monsters by putting salt on them, scaring things by sticking your tongue out, etc.) Encourage her/him to think about this changed version of the bad dream as s/he falls asleep each night.

{My Story}

Objective: To desensitize the child(ren) to painful feelings surrounding traumatic events

Have the child identify something that happened that made him/ her feel very afraid. Ask the child to a write story about what happened. This could be a simple narrative, a picture book, etc. Make sure if you see any untrue or unhelpful thoughts or beliefs (like "It was my fault" or "Things will never get better") in the narrative to discuss them with the child and challenge him/her to replace the thoughts with more helpful ones. Have the child read and reread the story to you about 10 times. This will help to desensitize the child to the painful feelings associated with the story.

Due to the sensitive nature of information that may be included in the children's stories, this activity should not be used in a group setting. If you are usually seeing children in group, we suggest meeting with group members individually one or two times to complete this activity.

Follow-up: Have the child identify on a scale of 1-10 how afraid s/ he felt when thinking about this event *before* s/he started reading the story and then identify on a scale of 1-10 how afraid s/he feels *now* when thinking about this event. If the number has not decreased in severity, ask the child to continue reading the story over and over again until the number of severity decreases.

{Relaxation Story}

Objective: To provide the child(ren) with a coping skill for dealing with memories of traumatic events

Have the child identify a traumatic event and name it (i.e., when my dad was arrested, when mom got hurt, etc.) Have the child say the name of the traumatic event and then read this story aloud doing the exercises each three times. At the end of the story, have him/ her repeat the name of the traumatic event again. Repeat the whole process two or three times.

For group activity, have each child either name his/her traumatic event aloud or just think about it. Read the story aloud and do the actions together.

George's Relaxing Day

Once upon time, a boy named George went to a fair. George was a strange boy who always liked to copy what he saw. George saw some turtles at the petting zoo and ran up to pet one. The turtle got scared and stuck his head inside his shell. George tucked his head in his shoulders like a turtle, too.

Direct the child(ren) to do this by trying to touch his/her shoulders to his/her ears.

George got thirsty, so he went to the lemonade stand. He saw a woman making lemonade, so he pretended to make lemonade.

Direct the child(ren) to squeeze his/her hands like s/he is juicing lemons.

Next George went to watch the strongman flex his muscles. George stood in front of everyone and squeezed his muscles like they were huge. The crowd roared with laughter when they saw him.

Have the child(ren) flex his/her arm muscles like a strongman.

George got embarrassed and ran away from the crowd. He saw a clown balancing on stilts.

Tell the child(ren) to balance on his/her tip toes and take a few steps.

George looked over and saw a boy sneaking in through a skinny hole in the fence. The boy had to make his stomach as small as possible to get through the hole. George copied him, of course.

Have the child(ren) make his/her stomach small.

Finally, he went to look at the animals. He was excited to see a tiger, but the tiger looked very sleepy and let out a big yawn. George yawned, too.

Have the child(ren) stretch his/her mouth big like the tiger.

On his way home from the fair, George saw a man making a funny face. George laughed at him and realized he had a fly on his nose and was trying to get it off. George made a funny face like the silly man.

Tell the child(ren) to pretend there is a fly on his/her nose and try to get it off.

George had a relaxing day at the fair.

The End.

Follow-up: Ask the child(ren) to discuss how they felt before, after, and during the relaxation exercise. Ask her/him if s/he feel the same way about the traumatic event after having done this exercise.

Reproducible Worksheets

Reproducible Worksheet 5.1, *Seeing the Arrest*, acknowledges that children who witnessed their parents' arrests may have felt traumatized by the experience. The worksheet asks them to identify feelings and questions they may have had at the time. Allowing children to remember the arrest and the accompanying feelings may help in desensitizing them to the trauma.

Reproducible Worksheet 5.2, *Looking at Distressing Situations*, lists various traumatic situations and asks children to identify the ones they have experienced. They are then asked to rate how upset they were on a scale of 1-10. Admitting to traumatizing events is a first step in reprocessing those events and becoming desensitized to their traumatic impact.

Reproducible Worksheet 5.3, *Pushing out Pushy Thoughts*, uses cognitive theory to help children push out intrusive thoughts by replacing them with more positive thoughts. The visual image of this worksheet may also be helpful as children imagine their intrusive thought as small and their deliberate positive self-talk as big.

Reproducible Worksheet 5.4, *Changing Bad Dreams*, helps children to think differently about their nightmares by re-scripting them using funny and heroic endings. This is an important nightmare intervention used even with combat veterans with PTSD (Forbes, Phelps, McHugh, Debenham, Hopwood, & Creamer, 2004). It is suggested facilitators encourage children to continue discussing alternative endings for their nightmares.

Reproducible Worksheet 5.5, *Handling Emotions*, acknowledges many of the feelings traumatized children feel. It asks children to match up feelings descriptions with feelings words and then to identify a coping strategy. Because traumatized children have numbed some of their emotional responses, it is important to assist them in connecting labels of feelings with body sensations and developing a repertoire of coping strategies.

Seeing the Arrest

Sometimes children are around when their parent is arrested. If you saw your parent being arrested, you may have had lots of questions and lots of feelings. Circle the feelings and the questions you had. Write in any others you can think of.

confused   scared

embarrassed

angry   exposed

cheated

offended   defenseless

weak

insulted

hurt   ashamed   powerless

others? _____

Why do the police have to use handcuffs?

Why does s/he have to go right now?

How long is s/he going to be gone?

Who is going to take care of me?

Will I ever see her/him again?

Where are they taking her/him?

What is the "right to remain silent?"

Other? _____

Looking at Distressing Situations

Sometimes kids go through very upsetting situations (not your fault, by the way). Listed below are some upsetting situations. Circle YES or NO under each item if it has happened to you. If you circled YES, go to the 1-10 line and put a mark on the line above the number that measures how upset you were when this happened (1 = not upset; 10 = most upset).

1. Seeing or hearing a parent use drugs

    YES   NO   _____
                             1   2   3   4   5   6   7   8   9   10

2. Seeing or hearing other people use drugs

    YES   NO   _____
                             1   2   3   4   5   6   7   8   9   10

3. Seeing or hearing a parent get hit or beat up

    YES   NO   _____
                             1   2   3   4   5   6   7   8   9   10

4. Seeing or hearing other people get hit or beat up

    YES   NO   _____
                             1   2   3   4   5   6   7   8   9   10

5. Seeing or hearing a parent threatened with a weapon

    YES   NO   _____
                             1   2   3   4   5   6   7   8   9   10

6. Seeing or hearing other people threatened with a weapon

    YES   NO   _____
                             1   2   3   4   5   6   7   8   9   10

7. Knowing someone who died

    YES   NO   _____
                             1   2   3   4   5   6   7   8   9   10

8. Seeing or hearing people doing grown up things with their bodies

    YES   NO   _____
                             1   2   3   4   5   6   7   8   9   10

9. Being hit by a grown-up

    YES   NO   _____
                             1   2   3   4   5   6   7   8   9   10

10. Being forced to do things that made me feel uncomfortable

    YES   NO   _____
                             1   2   3   4   5   6   7   8   9   10

Pushing out Pushy Thoughts

Sometimes when bad things have happened to people, they can have thoughts that are intrusive or pushy. In other words, you could be doing your homework or eating dinner, and all of a sudden, a bad thought pops into your head. One way to push back on pushy/intrusive thoughts is to think about something you are enthusiastic about. Because you cannot think of two things at the same time, the enthusiastic thought will chase out the pushy/intrusive thought!

Write down one of your pushy/intrusive thoughts in small letters inside the small thought bubble below. Then write down a happy, enthusiastic thought in larger letters in the large thought bubble.

Changing Bad Dreams

Children who have a parent in jail sometimes have
bad dreams. This is understandable. But it can be
very uncomfortable – and it can rob you of a good
night's sleep! A good way to take care of these bad
dreams is to change the endings of them while you
are awake. Complete the sentences below.

My bad dream starts out as _____

_____ .

But then it turns bad when _____

_____ .

If I imagined something funny happening in this dream, it would be _____

_____ .

And then the dream would end with_____

_____ .

If I imagined being a hero in this dream, I would _____

_____ in it.

And then the dream would end with _____

_____ .

Handling Emotions

When children have experienced several bad things in their lives, it can make it hard for them to handle feelings/emotions. Learning to handle feelings/emotions starts with understanding what the feelings are and then finding ways to calm them. Look at the feeling descriptions on the left; match them to the feeling word in the center of the page by drawing a line to it; then find a good coping skill on the right and draw a line from the feeling word to the coping skill. You can use more than one coping skill, and you can use the same coping skill for several different emotions. One is done for you.

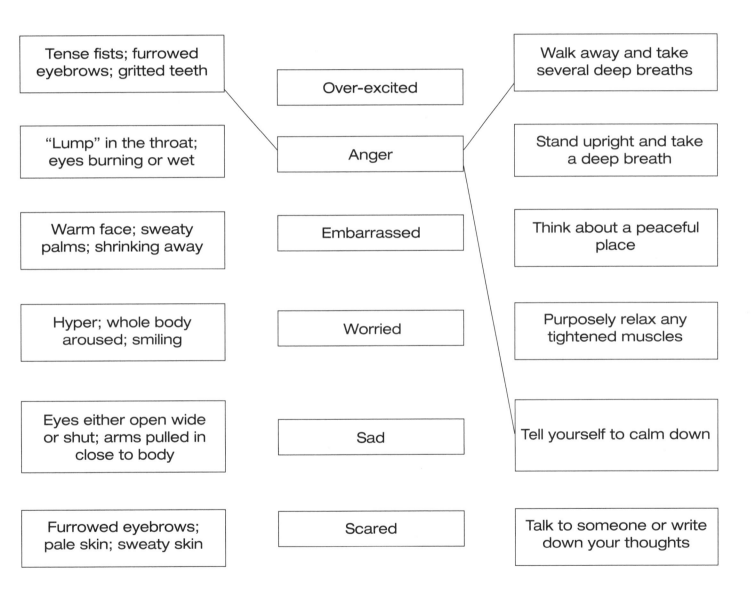

Lesson 6
Developing a Positive Identity

Notes to Facilitator

Children of incarcerated parents are 5-6 times more likely than their peers to enter the criminal justice system themselves (Miller, 2006). Murray, Janson, and Farrington (2007) found from a review of the literature that there is an independent effect of parental incarceration on children's antisocial behavior. One explanation for this phenomenon is what Murray Bowen (1978) called the intergenerational transmission process, or the transmission of patterns of functioning from one generation to the next. This transmission occurs on multiple levels from the conscious teaching and learning of information to a more psychological/emotional identification with family members.

The fact children of incarcerated parents are at higher risk than other children for incarceration themselves suggests that children's identity and sense of self may be strongly connected to a community where there is frequent illegal activity. In forming an identity, children try to think, act, and feel like significant people in their social environment. They also take in the available information around them.

Erikson (1968) described identity as a multifaceted system of self-definition formed within a social context that provides explanation for life experiences and helps to guide life choices. Not surprisingly, research has shown there are strong links between identity and psychological health. Indeed, one's identity or sense of self helps to enhance motivation and regulate behaviors which subsequently affect self-esteem (Yowell, 2000).

In order to provide positive information for children to internalize, it is important for significant people in a child's life to provide feedback to the child about his/her strengths, positive behaviors, and overall worth as a person (Harter, 1998; Katz, 1996). This is particularly true for children of incarcerated parents because the shame and stigma associated with having an incarcerated parent can lead to feelings of inferiority and low self-esteem, thus making them vulnerable to developing a negative identity. Dubow, Arnett, Smith, and Ippolito (2001) suggest that optimism is also an important component for a positive self-concept. Dreyer (1994) emphasizes the importance of providing a supportive context for children to have choices and opportunities for self-exploration. The cyclical nature of intergenerational incarceration highlights the need for effective treatment to include positive identity formation for children of incarcerated parents.

> **The shame and stigma associated with having an incarcerated parent can lead to feelings of inferiority and low self-esteem, thus making them vulnerable to developing a negative identity.**

Suggestions:

» Help children set goals and then praise them for their *efforts* – not simply the outcomes.

» Give children choices and opportunities to make decisions. Teach children problem solving skills and point out times when they successfully solve a problem.

» When children make good choices or have successes, assist them in attaching these experiences to their identity by asking the question, "What do you think this says about you as a person?"

» Help children explore how they are alike and how they are different from one another and from members in their families.

» Teach and encourage optimism.

» Encourage children to think about and plan for the future.

Script

Just because you have a parent that went to jail or prison does not mean you will go to jail or prison when you grow up. It also does not mean you are a bad person. Everyone has things they are good at. Just like there are consequences for making bad choices, there are benefits of making good choices. When you do things you are good at, you may get things like rewards, positive attention, and good feelings. Setting goals and planning for the future is part of becoming a successful person. Trying things out like hobbies or different activities can help you find out what you are good at. Purposely thinking good thoughts about yourself can help you experience good feelings and do good things.

Prison Letters

Dear Alonzo,

Your mom just sent me a package and inside she sent me copies of some of your accomplishments. Counselors Honor Roll! I almost fell out of my chair when I saw that. I can't stop telling all the guys here how smart my son is. You are going to make something of yourself, I know it. Every Thursday I go talk to a counselor and a group of other inmates about our feelings and stuff. I brought that last picture you drew for me and passed it around. They all agree with me that you are a talented artist. Sometimes it has been hard for me to tell you with words what I think about you, but I want to make sure you know I think you are a great kid. I probably don't tell you that enough. If I could, I would stand on top of the tallest building with a microphone and tell the whole city my son is on the Counselor's Honor Roll. You should be proud of yourself. "

Love you, Dad

Questions:

1. Why do you think it is sometimes hard for Alonzo's dad to tell him how proud of him he is?

2. What are some things you have to be proud of?

3. If your parent were to write you a letter like this, what do you wish it would say?

Additional Discussion Questions

» Do you sometimes not get credit for good things you do because your parent is in jail? How did you deal with that?

» What do other people say you are good at?

» What is something you have done that you have been proud of?

» What is something you have succeeded at? What does that say about you?

» Who is someone you admire (or look up to)? How are you like that person?

» What kind of reputation would you like to have? What do you have to do to develop that kind of reputation?

Activities

{This is Me}

Objective: To identify positive attributes about the self

Cut out large font descriptive words such as smart, athletic, funny, creative, loving, etc. Have the child cut out pictures from magazines of things s/he likes or things that reminds him/her of things s/he is good at. Have child trace outlines of his/her body on butcher paper. Let the child paste pictures and descriptive words on the body to show all the good things about him/her.

For group activity, let each child decorate his/her own person.

Follow-up: Ask the child(ren) to share his/her project and identify feelings associated with focusing on what s/he is good at. Ask her/him to describe specific situations when s/he experienced these qualities.

{My Skills}

Objective: To improve feelings of competence

On separate sheets of paper, write out lots of things kids can do (skills and knowledges) such as write, sing, draw, throw a basketball, be kind to others, skip, know math facts, etc. Post these around the room and have the child go around and sign his/her name to each sheet that describes something s/he can do.

For group activity, have each child sign the papers that apply to each individual.

Follow-up: Summarize the skills that have been identified. Ask the child(ren) to name any other skills that were not posted. Discuss how the child(ren) learned these skills and the feelings associated with learning new skills.

{I am Competent}

Objective: To improve self-confidence

Teach the child a simple magic trick. Directions: Prearrange a deck of cards into two stacks (one stack of the black cards and one stack of the red cards). Have a spectator draw a card out of one of the piles without showing it to you. Allow the spectator to shuffle that card *into the other stack*. Always make sure the cards are kept face down. Once the card has been shuffled back in, the child can look through that stack and pick out the card. It will be the only card in that stack that is a different color!

For group activity, teach the trick to the group and let them partner up and practice with each other.

Follow-up: Discuss how it feels to learn new things; discuss how one has to sometimes stick with something for awhile to learn it (especially if it is difficult).

{Scrapbook}

Objective: To make a visual reminder of accomplishments

Give the child a disposable camera or use a digital camera. Have the child take pictures of his/her accomplishments and things s/he enjoys doing. Make a scrapbook with the pictures. If you need a less expensive activity, s/he could draw pictures, print pictures off the internet, bring pictures from home, or cut pictures from magazines, etc.

For group activity, allow each child to make his/her own scrapbook and then share it with the group.

Follow-up: Have the child(ren) share the scrapbook and discuss his/her accomplishments. If possible, have the child(ren) share the scrapbook with other adults.

{Autograph Book}

Objective: To receive affirmation from others

Fold several pieces of paper in half and staple together into a book. Let the child decorate the cover of the book. The child should get at least 6-8 people, such as teachers, friends, parents, etc., to sign the book and also write something they like about the child in the book.

For group activity, make the books during one session and then have them bring the books back signed the following session to share with the group. Group members can also sign each others' books.

Follow-up: Allow the child(ren) to share the book and discuss how it feels to read the affirming words from others. Ask the child(ren) where s/he will keep the book so that s/he can look at it in the future when feeling down.

{I'm too Good for That}

Objective: To practice resisting negative choices or negative peer pressure

Have the child role play several scenarios in which s/he is faced with a bad choice or negative peer pressure. Each time the child should answer, "I'm too good for that."

For group activity, have the children role play the different characters in the scenario, repeating until each person has had several turns refusing.

Scenario 1: The two boys in Billy's class that are usually mean to him want to play with him on the playground one day. Once they get outside, the two boys try and get Billy to smoke cigarettes with them.

Scenario 2: Sally hears from Jasmine that Stephanie wants to fight her after school because she stole her boyfriend. All the kids in Sally's class want to know if she is going to fight.

Scenario 3: Andre and his best friend Jeremy are at the grocery store. Andre keeps complaining he is hungry. Jeremy tells him to just shut up and steal a candy bar.

Follow-up: Discuss what consequences there could have been if the child(ren) had not made a good choice. Ask the child(ren) to discuss how it felt to successfully resist peer pressure. Compare times when it is easier and when it is harder to resist.

{Hot Seat (Group Activity)}

Objective: To improve feelings of belonging and self-worth

Have one person sit in the middle of a circle of children in the "Hot Seat." Have each person in the circle tell the person in the "Hot Seat" one thing s/he likes or appreciates about him/her. After each appreciation have the child in the "Hot Seat" say, "Thank you." Give each child a chance to have a turn in the "Hot Seat."

Follow-up: Allow children to discuss how it felt to hear others say good things about them. Ask them which things they agreed with and which ones they did not. Discuss the importance of saying, "Thank you" after receiving a compliment.

Reproducible Worksheets

Reproducible Worksheet 6.1, *I am Good*, asks children to identify their strengths by writing ways they are smart, personality characteristics they like about themselves, and skills they can perform. It is important for children to see their own strengths, skills, and assets and not simply identify with a troubled parent.

Reproducible Worksheet 6.2, *Self-Esteem Dice*, has children cut out and glue a paper dice together. They can then use the dice to create a game that helps children continue identifying ways in which they have been successful or helpful or loved.

Reproducible Worksheet 6.3, *Like and Different*, directs children to identify ways they are similar and different from their incarcerated parent. Transgenerational theory suggests that differentiating from one's family of origin is an important emotional task (Bowen, 1978; Carter & McGoldrick, 1989). While differentiating is a life-long endeavor, children of incarcerated parents may have difficulties separating themselves emotionally from family chaos and anxiety. Assisting them to see both similarities and differences with their incarcerated parent can aid in this process.

Reproducible Worksheet 6.4, *I am a Rule Follower*, asks children to name rules they are good at following. Recognizing their own positive behavior (and not focusing on problematic negative behaviors), children can see themselves as good kids. Seeing themselves as good people then has a positive influence on feelings, thoughts, conversations and behaviors (Jopling, 1997).

Reproducible Worksheet 6.5, *If I were a …*, encourages children to further develop their self-awareness by considering how they are like various objects (e.g., plant, animal, tool, etc.). Self-awareness is the cornerstone of emotional intelligence (Goleman, 1995) and while it is a life-long process, children can begin to look inward in order to better understand themselves, their feelings, drives, preferences, resources and intuitions.

Note: If you are doing this worksheet in a group, have everyone fold up their papers when they are finished and mix them up in a bowl. Then have each person pull one out and try to guess who it is!

Reproducible Worksheet 6.6, *Developing Hobbies*, asks children to review a list of hobbies and to check three they are most interested in. They are then directed to write down what they will need to develop these hobbies. Creating a positive identity includes investing in activities that are productive and pleasurable.

Reproducible Worksheet 6.7, *Putting Myself on the Line*, has several continuums with various trait dyads named at either end (e.g., shy----outgoing; still----active; careful----brave). Children are directed to put an "X" on the continuum at a place that describes where they see their personality on that particular trait. There is no right or wrong way of being. Children should be encouraged to accept themselves for who they are.

I Am Good!

Sometimes children who have a parent in jail think they are bad. This is simply not true! Using one of the bodies below as you, do the following:

1. Write on the forehead something you are smart at.
2. Write on the chest 2 things about your personality/character that is positive.
3. Write on the arms or legs 2 things you are good at doing.
4. Color the person to look like you!

Self-Esteem Dice

Directions: Cut out the figure below on the dotted lines. Fold on the solid lines and glue the blank portions, making sure they go into the inside of the dice. Roll the dice and talk about the statement that turns up for you.

Tell about a time when you did a good job with your school work.	**Tell about a time that someone told you that they loved you.**	**Tell about a time when you did a good job cleaning up.**
	Describe one of your best personality qualities.	
	Tell about a time when someone gave you a compliment.	
	Tell about a time that you did a good deed for someone else.	

Like and Different

All children are like their parents in some ways and different from their parents in some ways. Think about your parent in jail. What are some ways you want to be *like* this parent and what are some ways you want to be *different* from this parent?

Alike	Different
_____	_____
_____	_____
_____	_____
_____	_____
_____	_____
_____	_____
_____	_____
_____	_____
_____	_____
_____	_____

I Am a Rule Follower

Everyone in life has rules. Teachers have rules about what they have to teach; parents have rules about the way they are supposed to treat their kids; even policemen have rules about how they give tickets and make arrests. Rules help the world stay orderly and safe. In the spaces below, name some rules you are good at following at home and at school.

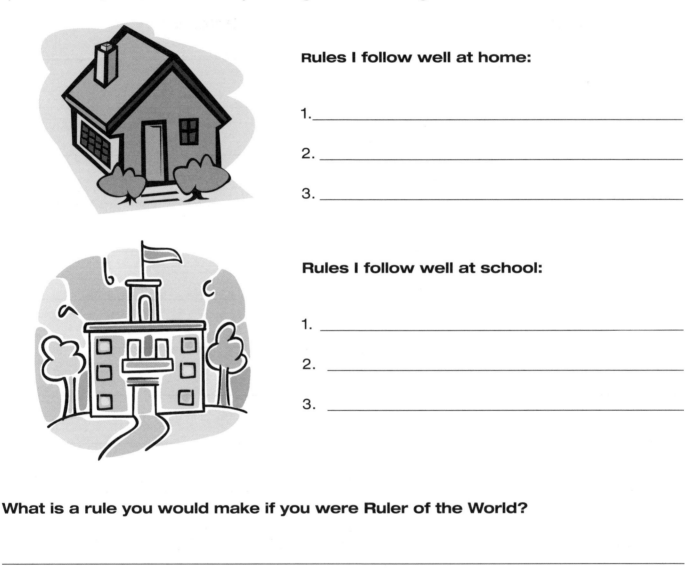

Rules I follow well at home:

1._____

2. _____

3. _____

Rules I follow well at school:

1. _____

2. _____

3. _____

What is a rule you would make if you were Ruler of the World?

_____

_____

If I were a ...

All of us are different. All of us have unique personalities and opinions. Read the following sentence starters and complete each one with a word that best fits you.

1. If I were an animal, the animal that would best describe my

   personality is a _____.

2. If I were a tool, the tool that would best describe my

   personality is a _____.

3. If I were a plant, the plant that would best describe my personality is a

   _____.

4. If I were a building, the building that would best describe my personality is a

   _____.

5. If I were a piece of furniture, the piece of furniture that would best describe my personality

   is a _____.

Developing Hobbies

It's great to have hobbies and interests. It's part of who we are. Listed below are several hobbies and interests. Add some of your own ideas and then check three (3) you might be most interested in. At the bottom of the page, write down what you need to further develop these hobbies.

❑ Collecting stamps

❑ Collecting cards

❑ Playing baseball

❑ Playing football

❑ Playing volleyball

❑ Doing karate or Tae Kwon Do

❑ Cooking

❑ Knitting/crocheting

❑ Playing an instrument

❑ Training animals

❑ Collecting figurines

❑ Collecting coins

❑ Playing basketball

❑ Playing soccer

❑ Bowling

❑ Playing golf

❑ Sewing

❑ Painting

❑ Writing stories or poetry

❑ Reading

_____

_____

_____

_____

What do you need to be able to become more involved in these activities?

_____

_____

Putting Myself on the Line

All of us are a mix of lots of different traits and qualities. Think about your personality and then look at the lines below. Each line has two "ends" of a particular quality. Put an "X" on the spot on the line where you think you fall on each of the scales. For example, if you are not particularly shy or outgoing you would put your "X" in the center. If you are bit more shy than you are outgoing, you would put your "X" slightly left of the center and if you are very shy, you would put your "X" way to the left of the line.

SHY --- OUTGOING

STILL --- ACTIVE

CAREFUL --- BRAVE

QUIET --- LOUD

HEALTHY --- UNHEALTHY

CHEERFUL -- SAD

SMART --- FOOLISH

CREATIVE -- BLAND

MUSICAL --- TONE DEAF

IDLE -- DILIGENT

Lesson 7
Learning to Ensure Success

Notes to Facilitator

Research shows between 42% and 70% of incarcerated parents do not have a high school education (Banauch, 1985; Mumola, 2000; Snell, 1994). If one of the strongest indicators of academic success is parent involvement/parent motivation (as research suggests — e.g., Bowen & Bowen, 1998a), children of incarcerated parents are at a huge disadvantage. They have few role models who can exhibit enthusiasm about learning. Indeed, several researchers have identified a drop in school work from children of incarcerated parents (Jucovy, 2003; Lowenstein, 1986). Staton (1980) found that children whose mothers were in jail performed more poorly academically than children whose mothers were on probation.

This is well known to caregivers. A 1993 study done by the National Council on Crime and Delinquency found that caregivers of children whose parents were incarcerated identified learning/school as their biggest concern (as quoted in Simmons, 2000). Poor concentration, poor motivation, and behavioral problems all contribute to the problem. Furthermore, students may have difficulty concentrating due to intrusive thoughts from trauma. Anxiety and stress affect academic performance because intrusive thoughts and worry compete with the limited processing resources of working memory (Eysenck & Calvo, 1992). Feeling unsafe and hypervigilant means students are not able to attend to learning.

Research shows that students who are more engaged in school do better academically. Student engagement is created when there is a school climate of belonging, when there are positive teacher-student relationships and where students have positive school-based peer relationships (Finn & Rock, 1997; Juvonen, 2006). Students are also more academically successful when they attend school regularly, complete required work both in and out of school, and participate in extracurricular activities – even when they are members of at-risk groups (Finn & Rock, 1997). Attention is also an important factor in students' academic success. Indeed, in Finn, Pannozzo, and Voelkl's research (1995), it was found that while both disruptive behavior and inattentive behavior were associated

> **Children of incarcerated parents have few role models who can exhibit enthusiasm about learning.**

with lower achievement scores, inattentive students did even more poorly than the disruptive students.

In Richard Lavoie's book, *The Motivation Breakthrough: 6 Secrets for Turning on the Tuned-Out Child,* six motivational strategies are identified that stimulate academic engagement. They are praise, power, projects, people, prizes and prestige. Students vary in what motivates them, so it is important to assess a child's "motivational style." According to Lavoie (2008), students who like status or recognition will be particularly motivated by praise and verbal attention; students who are insistent

or aggressive may be motivated by power (opportunities to be in control); students who are inquisitive may be motivated by projects (rather than just written assignments); students who are very social may be motivated by connections and people in their lives (having special relationships with teachers or mentors); students who like status and possessions may be motivated by prizes and, finally, students who need to feel special or important may be motivated by prestige or recognition (i.e., showcasing their talents).

Suggestions:

» Assist teachers in creating classrooms and playgrounds where students feel safe, secure and calm.

» Determine students' motivational styles and share that information with caregivers and teachers in order to better engage them in school work.

» Encourage teachers to create positive one-on-one relationships with students of incarcerated parents. Grades and academic motivation are higher among students who report higher levels of teacher support (Bowen & Bowen, 1998b).

» Help children develop better attention skills, social skills, and impulse control.

» Connect children to appropriate extracurricular activities at school.

» Help children develop good study habits at home.

» Connect students to academic mentors. Mentored students have fewer unexcused absences, better attitudes and behaviors at school (Herrera, Sipe, & McClanahan, 2000).

Script

Doing your best in school is one way to work towards having a successful future. Everyone has different ways of learning, but things like good study skills can be learned. Kids who have a parent in jail sometimes have difficulty concentrating on school work because they are distracted by their problems. This means it is very important for you to pay extra attention to being a successful student. Paying attention in class, following directions, and trying your best are important parts of being successful in school. It is also important to know when and who to ask for help when you need it.

Prison Letters

Dear Dad,

Grandma is making me write you this to tell you I got a D in Social Studies on my progress report. I hope you are not too mad at me. I already know what you are going to say – school is the key to success; it doesn't matter what your grades are as long as you have tried your best and I know your best is not a D and I won't get to play my video games after school if my grades start slipping. It is just so hard to pay attention sometimes. I find myself daydreaming and thinking about you, wondering what you are doing, and wishing you were home. My teacher, Ms. Newman, says I just need to focus more. She even gave me a rubber band to wear on my wrist. I can snap it to remind myself to pay attention if my mind starts wandering. I guess I better go do my homework. I promise I will do my best to get my grade up.

Love, Alonzo

Questions:

1. Why do you think Alonzo's dad believes that school is the key to success?

2. What do you think would help Alonzo focus better in Social Studies class?

3. Do you ever find yourself thinking about your problems when you are supposed to be thinking about your school work?

Additional Discussion Questions

» Do you have trouble paying attention in school? What happens when you try to focus on something?

» How do you feel when you don't know what is going on?

» What can you do when you feel your mind start to wander?

» What is your favorite part of going to school?

» Describe a time when you did well in a subject. What do you think helped you to be successful?

» Who is an adult at school who you feel comfortable asking help from?

Activities

{Listen and Follow Directions}

Objective: To improve listening skills and focus

Give each child a piece of paper and something to write with. Read the following directions out loud to the child. When you are finished, the child will end up with a drawing of something if s/he has followed the directions. Explain s/he will have to listen closely and pay attention because you will only read the directions one time.

1. Draw a backward C in the middle of the page. Now draw a 2-inch line going straight up from the top left edge of the C. At the top of that line, draw a 2-inch line going to the right.

The child should end up with a drawing of the number 5.

2. Draw a 2-inch line from left to right. At the end of the first line, draw a 2-inch line going straight up. From the end of that line, draw a 2-inch line going to the left. Now from the end of that line, draw a triangle that connects the top of the two vertical lines together with the bottom line of the triangle.

The child should end up with the shape of the house.

For a group activity, have all the children listen and draw the pictures.

Follow-up: Discuss what was easy and what was difficult about the activity. Ask the child(ren) how s/he got her/his mind to pay attention if it started to drift.

{Memory Game}

Objective: To improve memory and concentration

Explain to the child that to win this game, s/he will have to be careful to focus and remember what s/he sees. Have 3-10 items (depending on the age and ability of the child) setting on a table covered with a cloth or sheet. Give the child 2-3 minutes to look and try to memorize what s/he sees, and then cover the items again. Once time is up, have the child make a list of all the items s/he can remember.

For group activity, have each child make a list of the items s/he can remember. Whoever remembers the most items wins.

Follow-up: Ask the child(ren) to name times when concentration is important. Discuss strategies s/he has used to improve memory and concentration.

{Self-Control Race}

Objective: To allow child(ren) to focus on slowing down instead of rushing through things

Put a piece of tape on the ground for a starting line and another piece of tape about 15 feet away. Have the child stand behind the first line and explain to him/her the goal is to concentrate on walking slowly and to cross the second line in exactly one minute. S/he is not allowed to stand still or move backwards.

For group activity, have the children line up behind the first line like they are going to race. Explain the rules about moving across the line in exactly one minute. Whoever crosses the line closest to one minute wins.

Follow-up: Ask child(ren) to discuss how doing things too quickly can be a problem. Discuss when it would be beneficial for her/him to slow down and do things more carefully.

{Bag of Tricks}

Objective: To identify strategies that will help child(ren) improve focus

Cut out the pictures from Appendix E or put something to represent the following items in a bag: glasses, headphones, hand, pencil and paper, bubbles, and question mark. Have the child draw the items (or slips of paper) out of the bag and describe how that item can represent a trick to help him/her focus. Expand on his/her ideas with the following:

- » **Glasses:** We need to look at the person who is talking. When our eyes wander, our brain wanders.
- » **Head Phones:** The radio is only tuned to one channel at a time. We need to use our ears to tune in to what the teacher is saying.
- » **Hand:** Raising your hand helps you to participate in class discussions or ask questions if you don't understand something.
- » **Pencil and Paper:** Taking notes while you are listening helps to stay focused.
- » **Bubbles:** You can pretend you are in a soundproof bubble that blocks out all the other extra noise and people in the room.
- » **Question Mark:** If you don't understand something, ask questions.

For group activity, have the children take turns pulling items out of the bag and describing how they think it could symbolize a way to help them focus.

Follow-up: Ask the child(ren) which strategy that they think would work best for her/him/them and why.

{The Last Thing I Said Game}

Objective: To improve listening skills.

Encourage the child to use the tricks from the last activity to play this game. Explain it is important to look at the person who is talking and to listen closely. Read a book or story to the child and tell her/him you are going to stop in the middle of a sentence. See if the child can tell you the last five words you read before stopping. Do this throughout the story.

For group activity, have the children raise their hand if they can tell you the last three words. For older children, you can have them write down the last five words. Check at the end to see who got the most right answers to find a winner.

Follow-up: Ask the child(ren) to discuss if and how s/he was able to use the tricks. If the child(ren) was successful, ask her/him what s/he thinks this success means about her/him as a person (i.e. "It means I am a good listener," "It means I know how to pay attention," etc.)

{Top Ten List}

Objective: To identify the importance of school and to improve academic motivation

Ask the child if s/he has ever paid attention to the top ten songs on the radio or the top ten movies at the box office. Have the child develop a top ten list of reasons why school is important. Encourage the child to think about these things when s/he is lacking motivation.

For group activity, come up with the ten reasons together. Write the list on a dry erase board, flip chart, or chalkboard, if available.

Follow-up: Allow child(ren) to discuss times/situations where s/he does and does not feel motivated at school.

Reproducible Worksheets

Reproducible Worksheet 7.1, *School Favorites,* asks children to identify some of the positive aspects of school. They are asked about favorite teachers, field trips, subjects, etc., in order to minimize any "awfulizing" about school in general. In order for children to develop positive attitudes about school, it is important for them to focus on the rewarding and enjoyable components of school! This is what Fredericks, Blumenfeld, and Paris (2004) describe as emotional engagement in school. Students who are emotionally engaged in school are more likely to remain in school.

Reproducible Worksheet 7.2, *How Do I Learn Best?,* asks children to consider their own learning style. They identify their best learning activities, their best learning spaces, their best motivational strategies, their best study environments, their best learning times, and favorite persons to ask for help. This is presented in a multiple choice format in order to assist children in considering various motivational/learning strategies. However, if children identify ways they learn best that are not listed, encourage them to add their own ideas! Helping children to understand their personal learning style and encouraging them to make use of this insight can optimize their study time and make them better students.

Reproducible Worksheet 7.3, *Roadblocks to Paying Attention,* lists ways children become distracted in the classroom and asks them to identify which distractions are most problematic for them. They are then asked to create a plan to address these "roadblocks" to attention. Before children can learn, they must be able to pay attention to lessons. Children of incarcerated parents can be distracted by internal worries/intrusive thoughts as well as external activities and noises. Addressing these distractions may help them attend to school work in more productive ways.

Reproducible Worksheet 7.4, *Study Habits,* invites children to assess their own study habits and to select one study habit they would like to work on. Some of the study habits that are described include having a special place to do homework, having a consistent time to do homework, spending time reading even when it is not assigned, setting academic goals, asking questions, etc. Good study practices make learning easier and more successful.

Reproducible Worksheet 7.5, *Impulse Control in the Classroom,* introduces children to the idea that impulses can cause problems in school. It asks them to stop and think about the consequences of certain impulses they might experience in school and to develop positive self-talk in order to make better choices. The scenarios include the impulse to cheat, the impulse to begin work without listening to the instructions, and the impulse to play outside rather than do homework. Being a good student often means delaying gratification.

Reproducible Worksheet 7.6, *Listening to Directions,* explains students are more successful when they listen to directions. It directs children to read over several scenarios where children are either following directions or not following directions and to identify the ones that are following directions. As many teachers can verify, following instructions is the first step to being successful with work!

School Favorites

Sometimes kids complain about school, but there are many wonderful things about going to school and learning. Think of some of these and write them in the spaces provided.

1. Who has been your favorite teacher?

    _____

    Why?

    _____

2. What is your favorite subject?

    _____

    Why?

    _____

3. What has been your favorite field trip?

    _____

    Why?

    _____

4. What is something you have learned at school that you have been able to talk about outside of school?

    _____

5. What class project or assignment have you been the proudest of?

    _____

How do I Learn Best?

Everyone learns differently. It is important to know your own personal learning style so you can be the best student you can be. Look at each of the questions below and circle the answer that best describes you.

1. I learn best by ...
    a. Reading or looking at it
    b. Hearing or talking about it
    c. Writing about it
    d. Touching or moving it

2. I learn best by ...
    a. Studying alone
    b. Studying with one other person
    c. Studying in a group

3. I learn best by ...
    a. Studying in complete silence
    b. Studying with some soft background music
    c. Studying with something to squeeze in my hands

4. I feel best about school and school work ...
    a. When I receive a lot of praise
    b. When I know lots of people at school
    c. When I can be in charge of something
    d. When I get rewards

5. I do a better job on my homework if I do it ...
    a. While I am still at school
    b. As soon as I get home
    c. After I have eaten something and relaxed for a few minutes
    d. After I have exercised

6. When I need help with my work, I can ask ...
    a. My teacher
    b. My caregiver
    c. A friend
    d. A neighbor or mentor

Roadblocks to Paying Attention

There are lots of "roadblocks" (things that get in the way) to paying attention in school. Look at the list of problems that get in the way of paying attention on the left. Decide which three (3) you have the most trouble with and write those on the roadblock signs on the right. Then answer the question below.

Feeling confused about the work

Daydreaming

Getting distracted by others around me

Wanting to be silly

Feeling bored

Thinking about my parent in jail

Remembering things I don't like to remember

Worrying

Thinking about what I am going to do after school

What is your plan for removing these roadblocks so you are able to pay good attention?

_____

_____

Study Habits

Often times you can study more efficiently and learn more if you are organized. This means developing good study habits. Look at the list of good study habits below. Think about whether or not you practice these and circle TRUE if the statement is true for you and FALSE if it is false for you. Then look at the FALSEs and select one you would like to work on. Write it at the bottom of the page.

Rather than doing homework just anywhere, I have a special homework "zone" where I do my homework.

TRUE   **FALSE**

I have a consistent time set aside for doing homework.

TRUE   **FALSE**

I spend time reading even if it is not a part of my homework.

TRUE   **FALSE**

I have files or folders or sections of notebooks specifically marked for each different subject. I organize all of my work in these.

TRUE   **FALSE**

I set academic goals for myself at the beginning of each school year.

TRUE   **FALSE**

I ask questions and seek help when I do not understand something or when I need assistance.

TRUE   **FALSE**

I make and use flashcards to study facts.

TRUE   **FALSE**

I make sure I read the instructions before starting any test or assignment.

TRUE   **FALSE**

After reviewing some of the good study habits above, what is one thing you are willing to work on?

_____

_____

Impulse Control in the Classroom

Sometimes students have feelings and urges (called impulses) to do things that are not very helpful, but they do them anyway because they do not stop and think about the consequences (what will happen). Read the situations below and write inside the thought bubbles what these students should tell themselves.

Natasha did not study for her spelling test. Now she has the impulse to copy John's answers. What should she tell herself?

Cameron's teacher is passing out papers, markers, and scissors. Cameron has the impulse to start cutting before he hears the teacher's instructions. What should he tell himself?

Jeremiah can only play outside when it is light out, and he LOVES to play outside. There is only one hour left of sunshine when he gets home from school, and he has a lot of homework to do. The rule at his house is "Homework before play." He has the impulse to tell his caregiver he doesn't have any homework. What should he tell himself?

Listening to Directions

Students are more successful when they listen to directions. That's because they can do the assignment correctly! Look at the students below. Some of them are following directions and some are not. Write who is listening to directions on the awards below.

 Samantha read pages 12-14. The teacher told the class to read pages 12-14.

 Bayley wrote a paragraph on the computer, but she turned off the computer without saving her work. The teacher told the class to save their work so they could add to it tomorrow.

 Paul finished his math assignment by using addition on all of the problems. The teacher said to add all of the problems.

 Jeremy was the first one finished with his work, but no one could read it. The teacher said to write in their neatest handwriting.

 Hazem looked up dinosaurs on the internet. The teacher said to get information on a subject that students were interested in.

 Julie did all the even problems on page 31 in math. The teacher said to do all the odd problems on page 31.

Lesson 8
Handling Angry Feelings

Notes to Facilitator

Children of incarcerated parents often exhibit both internalizing and externalizing behaviors. These may include depression and attachment difficulties as well as anger and disruptive/delinquent behaviors (Travis, 2005). In addition to fear, guilt, grief, rejection, shame, and loneliness, feelings of anger are quite common (Gabel, 1992; Greene, Haney, & Hurtado, 2000). Anger towards an incarcerated parent is a legitimate and reasonable feeling. Children may feel angry for the criminal involvement itself, or they may feel angry for the lifestyle adjustments the incarceration has brought, or they may feel angry about the shame they feel with extended family members and peers. Their anger is often displayed in acting out behaviors (Jucovy, 2003).

Angry feelings may surface or they may be internalized from others' expressed anger towards the incarcerated parent. It is quite common for the incarcerated parent and current caregiver of the child to have experienced conflicts in their relationship prior to the incarceration. Children may hear these caregivers speaking negatively about their incarcerated parent. Children in foster care also may be privy to negative conversations about the incarcerated parent. Angry feelings from these children may be directed specifically at individual family members, or they may be more generalized as aggression and/or a "bad attitude."

Research has shown that cognitive-behavioral interventions significantly reduce anger (Deffenbacher, Lynch, Oetting, & Kemper, 1996). Indeed, the way someone thinks about an anger-producing event shapes the level of anger s/he experiences. Research has shown reappraisal of anger-promoting cognitions can change the affective response (Ray, Wilhelm, & Gross, 2008). This can be done intrapersonally or interpersonally. Classic cognitive therapy involves identifying, challenging, and changing cognitive distortions. An interpersonal version of this was discussed by Davidson, MacGregor, Stuhr, Dixon, & MacLean (2000) and included working with another person to explore various causes for the anger-triggering event. This helped the angry person appreciate the complexity of the situation, thereby leading to different interpretations and ultimately decreasing angry feelings. Similarly, children of incarcerated parents can benefit from others' assistance in gaining different perspectives regarding daily anger-producing events.

> **Research has shown that cognitive-behavioral interventions significantly reduce anger.**

Suggestions:

» Assist children in realizing they can have mixed feelings for an incarcerated parent. Assure them they can both love and feel angry towards the same person.

» Assure children angry feelings are OK. Nonetheless, it is important for children to learn ways to express angry feelings that do not hurt themselves, others, or property.

» Children of incarcerated parents should be empowered to ask caregivers not to speak negatively about their parent in the same way children of divorced parents are encouraged to ask their parents not to speak disparagingly about one another.

» Anger may help otherwise powerless children to feel more powerful. Talk to children about healthier ways to feel powerful besides anger.

» Anger can also be learned. If there is domestic violence or abuse in the family, work with caregivers to manage their own anger challenges.

Script

Many children with a parent in prison have angry feelings. The way kids deal with their feelings of anger often leads to trouble. It is OK to get angry, but there are good and bad things you can do when you are angry. When you feel angry, it is good to do things like talk about your feelings, exercise, take a walk, take deep breaths, or express your feelings through art or writing. It is not OK to hurt yourself, other people, or property when you are angry. You can be better prepared to deal with angry feelings in a good way if you know how your body tells you that you are angry. Many people with anger feel tension in their hands and arms, their face will get tight, they might feel hot, or their heart might start beating faster. When you feel these things start to happen, you can have a plan in place about how you are going to deal with your anger. Remember, everyone feels anger sometimes, but not everyone lets their anger get them into trouble.

Prison Letters

"Dear Alonzo,

I am so excited you will be coming to visit me in just two weeks! I am probably going to hug you so tight you won't be able to breathe. Things here are pretty much the same. I still show my group all the pictures you draw me.

I wanted to talk to you about something. When I talked to your grandma on the phone last night, she told me you got into another fight at school. I understand you feel angry a lot. I guess you feel upset about things going on with our family, and you are taking it out on kids at school. Fighting is not going to help, Son. It is only going to hurt you and others. I have a lot of opportunities here to get mad and fight, but I choose not to. Instead I just try and cool off when things get tense, and I lift weights to clear my head. I want you to find better ways to handle your anger from now on.

Dad

Dear Dad,

I was hoping grandma wouldn't tell you about the fight. This kid just called mom a crack head for no reason. I know it was silly. Mom would never use crack. I just lost it. In some ways it felt good to fight. I have been feeling angry a lot lately. Even little things make me angry. Ms. Wells says other feelings I am having are making me feel angry. She says I need to talk about my feelings instead of hurting people. I have started drawing a lot more, and I think that is one way I can get my feelings out. One thing is for sure, the fight was not worth it. Grandma took away my PlayStation®, and I can't even watch TV anymore after 8 o'clock. I am glad you don't get in fights there. I worry about you getting hurt a lot. Well, I guess I will go stare at the wall since I can't watch TV!"

Love, Alonzo

Questions:

1. What could Alonzo have done instead of fighting?
2. What do you think Ms. Wells means when she says other feelings are making Alonzo angry?
3. How can drawing help Alonzo with his feelings?

Additional Discussion Questions

» What is something you feel angry about?

» What is something mean that has been said to you about your parent? How did you feel? What did you do?

» How can you tell when you are mad? What happens in your body?

» What are some OK ways and not OK ways to let your anger out?

» Who can you talk to in order to calm down when you are feeling mad?

Activities

{Levels of Anger}

Objective: To help the child(ren) understand that there are different levels of anger

Prior to the activity, search for 5-10 pictures of angry people online. Print and cut out the pictures. Explain to the child there are different levels of anger that require different types of responses. When you are the most angry, you have to be the most careful to stop and think in order not to do something that will get you into trouble. Have the child put the pictures in order from the least angry to the angriest.

For group activity, have the children discuss with each other why they think the pictures should go in that order and let them come to decisions as a group.

Follow-up: Have the child(ren) identify things that make her/him feel a little angry, a medium amount of angry, and very angry.

{Anger in My Body}

Objective: To recognize how anger feels physically

Read the list of body parts. Have the child stand up and show with his/her body and then describe with words how this body part feels when s/he is angry. Then ask him/her to show the difference between how the body parts feel when they are just a little angry or really furious.

Forehead	Heart	Stomach
Eyes	Arms	Cheeks
Mouth	Hands	Legs

For group activity have the children take turns showing and describing how anger feels in their bodies.

Follow-up: Discuss the unique ways the child(ren) feels her/his own anger. Discuss how recognizing anger in the body will help in using coping skills for anger.

{Dealing with Anger Scavenger Hunt}

Objective: To learn from adults various strategies for coping with anger

Give the child a copy of Anger Scavenger Hunt Handout in Appendix F. Have the child interview four different adults to ask the adults how they cope with anger. The child should take notes and then share what s/he found out with the facilitator. Depending on the setting, this can be done during the session or as homework.

For group activity, children can go as partners to interview the adults and share results with the group.

Follow-up: Ask the child(ren) to discuss what s/he learned and if s/he thinks any of the identified strategies might be helpful.

{Anger Role Play}

Objective: To practice appropriate ways of handling anger

Ask the child to share a time s/he felt angry and did something that was hurtful. Have the child role play the scenario, but *this time* have her/him act out a way s/he could have handled her/his anger appropriately. For example, Jake might describe the time that he hit his brother for playing in his room without asking. In the role play, instead of hitting his brother, he would tell the brother he feels angry and then go for a walk to cool off, take deep breaths, etc.

For group activity, ask one member of the group to share a time s/he felt angry. Other members of the group play characters in the scenario that have better ways the anger could have been handled.

Follow-up: Allow the child(ren) to identify benefits of handling anger appropriately. Ask her/him for examples of when s/he *has* handled angry feelings appropriately.

{Problem Balloons}

Objective: To externalize problems with anger and to utilize problem solving skills

Blow up several balloons. Direct the child to write some problems s/he has been having with anger on the balloons (one problem per balloon). When there are several problems on the balloons, pick up one balloon at a time and read the problem written on it. Have the child identify 2-3 things s/he could do to solve the problem. Once s/he has identified 2-3 solutions, have him/her sit on or stomp the balloon.

For group activity, have the children each identify at least one problem and then take turns coming up with solutions and popping the balloons.

Follow-up: Ask the child(ren) to discuss how it felt to see his/her problem popped. Discuss why it is important to think of more than one solution for a problem.

{Angry UNO®}

Objective: To use self-talk to cope with anger

Play the game UNO® with some changes (see suggestions below). The game is designed to be a little more frustrating than usual. Explain when we start to get angry, we can use self-talk to calm ourselves down. Encourage the child to tell him/herself things like "Oh well, it's just a game," "I will do better next time," "I need to be a good sport even when I'm losing," etc. Children often get angry during this game, which provides an in-the-moment opportunity to work on anger management. Some suggestions for the modified UNO® rules are:

» If a child plays a SKIP card, s/he gets to choose anyone in the game to skip, not necessarily the next player.

» If a child plays a DRAW TWO or DRAW FOUR card, s/he gets to pick anyone in the game to draw the cards.

» If a child plays a REVERSE card, s/he gets to give one of his/her own cards to another player and reverse the direction of the game.

» If any child **complains**, the leader gives him/her two extra cards.

This could be done as an individual activity, but to increase the level of frustration of the game, give the child two more cards whenever they play a card numbered 2 or 8.

Follow-up: Discuss successes and challenges at coping with anger during the game.

Reproducible Worksheets

Reproducible Worksheet 8.1, *Feeling Anger in My Body*, allows children to identify body sensations that are cues for their angry feelings. Understanding body cues can help children develop better control over angry feelings as they feel these sensations and then implement various coping strategies. Examples of body sensations can include tension, stiffness, muscle aches, tightness, heart pounding or racing, rapid breathing, feeling hot or flushed, upset stomach, etc. It is important to note that not all children will have the same body cues, so facilitators should allow for variance.

Reproducible Worksheet 8.2, *Feelings Leading to Anger*, helps children to recognize anger often accompanies other primary feelings. They are asked to write down five (5) situations when they felt angry and to mark other feelings they may have experienced at those times (from a list). Children are then directed to see if there are themes in the kinds of feelings that trigger their anger. Again, this can help children be alert to those anger triggers by realizing the feelings that tend to turn to anger for them.

Reproducible Worksheet 8.3, *Angry Letter*, provides a template for children to write an angry letter to their parent who is incarcerated. It assures them they can both love and be angry with the same person. Facilitators should give careful consideration to what children do with these letters after they are written. Generally, it is not advised children mail these letters unless caregivers and the incarcerated parent are notified.

Reproducible Worksheet 8.4, *Ways to Calm My Anger*, asks children to draw four (4) pictures of themselves using specific strategies to calm anger, such as drawing an angry picture, playing a video game or watching TV, taking five (5) deep breaths, and walking it off. After children have completed their pictures, the facilitator should ask how the children think they might be more successful. Other ideas should also be discussed (e.g., thinking of a peaceful place, talking to an adult, punching a pillow, etc.). It is important for children to learn they can be the "boss" of their angry feelings.

Reproducible Worksheet 8.5, *Stinkin' Thinkin' can Lead to Anger*, explains to children that feelings of anger can come from negative thinking. It describes overgeneralization, "should" statements, and jumping to conclusions. The worksheet then asks them to identify these with several examples. Lastly, they are asked to write more positive self-statements.

Feeling Anger in My Body

In order to handle angry feelings in healthy ways, it is important to know what your body's anger signals are. Look at the body below and write down the signals that different parts of your body give you when you are feeling angry. Then go back and choose colors to express what you have written and color the part of the body with the color you have chosen.

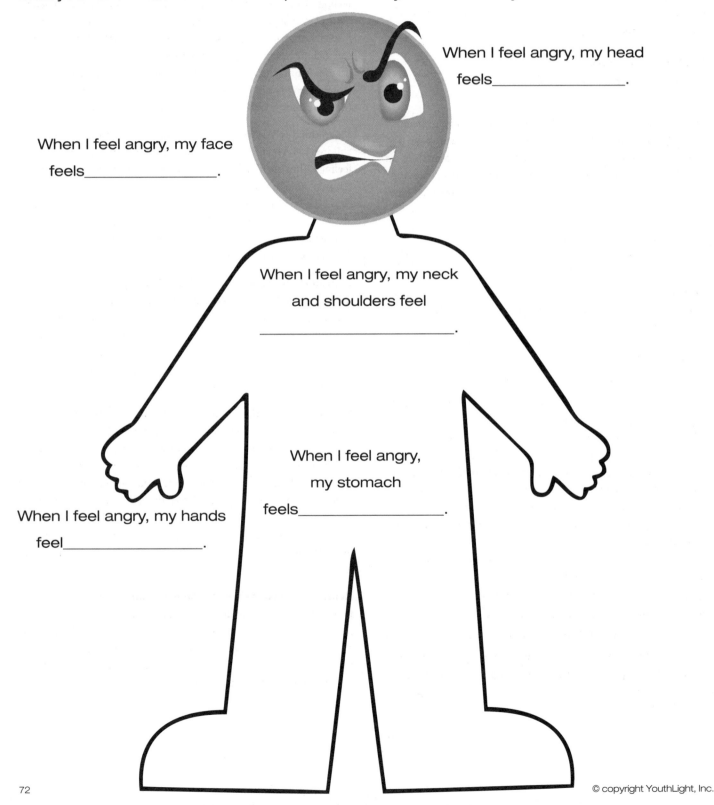

When I feel angry, my head feels_____.

When I feel angry, my face feels_____.

When I feel angry, my neck and shoulders feel _____.

When I feel angry, my stomach feels_____.

When I feel angry, my hands feel_____.

Feelings Leading to Anger

On the left hand side of the page, write down five (5) different times you have felt angry. This may have to do with your parent, or it may be something completely different. Then look at the feeling words listed at the top of the page and, in the boxes below the feeling words and across from the "Angry times," put checkmarks in the boxes under the feelings you felt with each incident. At the bottom of the page, add up your checkmarks in each column and discover which feeling(s) most frequently leads you to feeling angry!

Angry Times	Helpless	Disrespected	Stupid	Hurt	Picked on	Embarrassed	Worried
TOTALS							

Which feeling(s) leads you to anger the most often? _____

_____

Angry Letter

Sometimes you might feel angry with the parent who is in jail or prison. This is quite normal. Feeling angry with someone does not mean you don't love the person. It just means you don't like something s/he did or you wanted something s/he could not give you. It means your feelings of hurt, frustration, rejection, worry, helplessness, embarrassment or confusion led to angry feelings.

Sometimes it helps to let angry feelings out by using words. Finish the letter below. You don't have to send it. You can simply write down your feelings and then tear it up if you like!

Dear _____,

Sometimes I feel angry at you for _____

_____. It seems as if _____

_____

_____ .

I wish you would have _____

_____

_____ .

Some of my other feelings are _____

_____

_____ .

But just because I feel angry sometimes does not mean _____

_____

_____ .

I hope _____ .

Love,

Reproducible 8.4

Ways to Calm My Anger

Listed below are four ways to be the boss of your angry feelings so they are not the boss of you. Draw a picture of yourself doing each one.

Talking to a Caring Adult

Watching TV or Playing a Game

Walking It Off

Taking 5 Deep Breaths

Stinkin' Thinkin' can Lead to Anger

Feelings of anger can come from negative thinking - or "stinkin' thinkin'." Three kinds of "stinkin' thinkin'" are:

» Generalization: seeing a single bad situation as happening over and over again; uses phrases like "always" and "never" ("She never takes me anywhere.")

» Should statements: telling yourself that things ought or ought not to be the way you hoped or expected ("He shouldn't have stared at me.")

» Jumping to conclusions: thinking negatively without the facts ("She hates me.")

Read the situations below, identify the type of "stinkin' thinkin'" was used, and then write down what a more positive way of thinking would have been for each situation.

SITUATION
You and a friend are getting ready to play a board game and your friend shouts, "I get to go first!"

IDENTIFY THE STINKIN' THINKIN'
"He always gets to go first!"

_____

POSITIVE THINKING

_____

_____

SITUATION
Your caregiver lets your brother have the last piece of pie.

IDENTIFY THE STINKIN' THINKIN'
"She loves him more than me."

_____

POSITIVE THINKING

_____

_____

SITUATION
Your teacher told you to be quiet even though you weren't talking.

IDENTIFY THE STINKIN' THINKIN'
"She shouldn't accuse me like that!"

_____

POSITIVE THINKING

_____

_____

Lesson 9
Building Positive Relationships

Notes to Facilitator

There are many obstacles children of incarcerated parents face. As these children experience the shame and stigma associated with having a parent in prison or jail, they may withdraw socially or find less acceptance within their peer groups. Children who have been exposed to family violence or traumatic situations often exhibit elevated rates of behavioral and social problems. These problems may be externalized through acting out, aggression, etc., or internalized with depressed mood, withdrawal, shyness, etc. (Trocki & Caetano, 2003). Whether these behaviors are externalized or internalized, social skills deficits become evident (Mazza, 2006). Social skill deficits interfere with academic performance, social support, healthy emotional/functional adaptation, and self-esteem. Helping children to develop social skills and positive relationships can be invaluable in helping them navigate difficult times in their lives. Similarly, quality friendships have been demonstrated to serve as a protective factor for at risk children and a buffer against depressive tendencies (Miller & Coll, 2007).

What exactly are social skills? Social skills are those communication, problem-solving, empathic, and self-management abilities that allow someone to initiate and maintain positive interactions with others. They include skills such as greeting others, reading others' feelings, negotiating conflicts, having reciprocal conversations, joining in, showing an interest in others, inviting, cooperating, being assertive, etc. Just as athletic or artistic skills can be taught, learned, and improved; social skills can be learned and improved as well.

Perhaps the most important aspect of helping children to develop positive relationships is to give them opportunities for social interaction. According to Miller and Coll (2007), "Many aspects of social functioning are learned through social activities." Providing children with opportunities to engage in joint-task activities with peers has been shown to increase positive social interactions.

> **Perhaps the most important aspect of helping children to develop positive relationships is to give them opportunities for social interaction**

Socially withdrawn children who were simply given time to play games with other more socially developed children showed significant improvement in their social interactions (Gross, Messer, & Morris, 1995). Peers can model positive social behaviors and also provide reinforcement for appropriate social interactions. Play dates, involvement in extra-curricular activities, and other opportunities for children to have positive social interactions are vital in helping children develop social skills.

Suggestions:

» Caregivers should be encouraged to regularly arrange opportunities for social interactions, such as play dates.

» Children with social skill deficits should be discouraged from simply playing solitary games (such as video games) and should be encouraged to develop interests where *others* are needed to play (e.g., chess, basketball, ping pong, etc.).

» Caregivers should be encouraged to speak openly about their own feelings and demonstrate their ability to regulate their feelings. For example, when they are angry, they should model how to handle anger appropriately by saying, "I am angry because _____."

» Social skills like joining in a game, asking for permission, apologizing, giving compliments, saying 'please and thank you', waiting your turn, following directions, etc., should be taught and role-played.

» Mentors, teachers, and counselors can be important resources in helping to teach children social skills. The more these behaviors are reinforced in different settings, the more the child will be conditioned to use them in peer relations.

Script

Making friends and being able to get along with others is an important part of being successful. Some important skills in getting along with others include caring about other people's feelings, knowing how to join other kids who are playing, being able to encourage others, sharing, being kind, and solving problems. Kids that learn friendly behaviors usually have more friends, get to do more fun things, and feel better about themselves.

Prison Letters

Dear Mr. King,

I am one of the counselors at Alonzo's school. I wanted to write you and tell you about some of the exceptional things Alonzo has been doing. Over the past several months, Alonzo and I have been spending time together in my office. This has given him an outlet to talk about his feelings, and I have seen some dramatic changes in him. I have known many families like yours who have gone through difficult times. Some children respond to those times with increasing anger and hopelessness. Others use the hard times as an opportunity to grow and become a better person. Alonzo has developed into a young man who is sensitive to the feelings of others. I have seen him reach out to other children who are hurting and offer them friendship and support. Recently, a new child moved to our school and was very nervous his first day. Alonzo reached out to him and included him at lunch as well as on the playground. I watched this with tears in my eyes. Alonzo has started finding healthy outlets for his anger, such as art and sports. He is a leader and encourages his friends to do the right thing. He has a great attitude most of the time, but is willing to admit when he has a bad day. You may not be able to be with your son right now, but you can take comfort in the fact you have raised him to be an exceptional person.

Sincerely,

Ms. Wells

Questions:

1. How do you think Alonzo's father's time in prison has helped to make Alonzo a more caring person?

2. What are some ways your parent's time in prison has changed you for better or for worse?

3. How do you think Alonzo's father felt when he got this letter?

Additional Discussion Questions

» Why are friends important?

» What is a nice thing you said to someone this week?

» Name two things you can say to someone you are trying to know better.

» What is one strength and one weakness you have as a friend?

» What do you look for in a friend?

» What are some good ways to handle conflict when you and a friend disagree?

» What keeps some kids from having friends?

Activities
{Friendly Behaviors}

Objective: To differentiate between behavior that is friendly and behavior that is unfriendly

Put two signs on the wall, one that says "Friendly Behaviors" and one that says "Unfriendly Behaviors." Cut the behaviors out of Appendix G and have the child draw the slips with the behaviors on them out of a bag. Have the child tape the behavior to either the friendly or unfriendly sign.

For group activity, have children take turns drawing the behaviors, reading them to the group, and picking which sign to tape it to.

Follow-up: Ask the child(ren) which of the unfriendly behaviors s/he has engaged in. What were the results? Ask the child(ren) which of the friendly behaviors s/he has engaged in. What were the results?

{Encouragement Hot Potato (Group Activity)}
Objective: To demonstrate that friends encourage each other

Have children sit in a circle to play hot potato. When the music stops, the person holding the ball has to say something encouraging to another person in the group and then pass them the ball. The person who was encouraged starts the game over again. (If it appears that anyone in the group is not receiving encouraging words, direct the child holding the ball when the music stops to say something encouraging to the person on her/his right and then pass her/him the ball to start the game again. Continue in this manner.)

Follow-up: Discuss how children felt when they heard encouraging words from their peers. Ask the children to identify times when they could say encouraging words to each other throughout the day.

{Friend Interview (Group Activity)}
Objective: To find things in common with other children in the group and to connect commonalities to making friends

Explain to children that part of forming relationships is finding things you have in common with someone. Have the kids split into pairs and interview each other to find out the following information:

How many brothers and sisters do you have?

What is your favorite color?

What is your favorite food?

What is your favorite school subject?

What are three things you like to do for fun?

What kind of music do you like?

(Feel free to add other questions)

Have the partners identify at least one thing they have in common. Each person can then tell the group about her/his partner and what the two of them have in common.

Follow-up: Discuss how it feels to find things in common with others. Ask children if they know what they have in common with others in the group.

{Have You Ever? (Group Activity)}
Objective: To develop empathy and find commonalities between peers

Put a piece of tape in the middle of the room. Have the children line up in two groups on either side of the line. Read the following questions (you may add your own questions as well). If a child answers yes to the question, they should walk up to the line. If the answer is no, they should not move to the line. The questions go from general to more personal. Make sure you set a few ground rules, like no one is able to laugh at anyone else for their answers, respect each others feelings, etc.

Have you ever flown on an airplane?

Have you ever played on a baseball team?

Have you ever watched Nickelodeon?

Have you ever stayed awake all night?

Have you ever pretended to be sick because you don't want to go to school?

Have you ever lost your temper?

Have you ever known someone who uses drugs?

Have you ever seen an adult in your family hit another adult in your family?

Have you ever had someone you loved die?

Have you ever worried about your parent who is in jail?

Follow-up: Discuss the activity and ask the children if it surprised them to find out what they did and didn't have in common with the rest of the group.

{The Golden Rule}
Objective: To identify ways to treat friends

The golden rule is to treat others the way you want to be treated. Use a dry erase board or piece of paper to make a list of ways the child would want to be treated by others.

For group activity, have each person contribute to the list and discuss each item on the list to point out any common discrepancies the group notices.

Follow-up: Talk about any discrepancies between the ways the child(ren) wants to be treated and the ways s/he treats others. Ask the child(ren) what kind things they could do for others.

Reproducible Worksheets
Reproducible Worksheet 9.1, *Putting Yourself in Someone Else's Shoes*, explains to children the meaning of empathy and gives them an opportunity to consider how a person of their choosing might feel in various situations. Empathy is considered a social emotion – the foundation of positive social interactions. It is the shared emotional state that allows people to connect. Children

of incarcerated parents may feel so overwhelmed with their own emotions, they do not allow themselves to feel others' feelings (Mazza, 2002), thereby making empathy training an important intervention.

Reproducible Worksheet 9.2, *Showing an Interest in Others*, directs children to identify specific statements or questions they can say to others to show they are interested in the other person's activities. Showing an interest in others is a key to social success as noted even in the early work of Dale Carnegie in his book *How to Win Friends and Influence People*. Carnegie (1936) stressed the importance of being genuinely interested in others, encouraging others to talk about themselves, and making the other person feel important.

Reproducible Worksheet 9.3, *Social Skills Tic-Tac-Toe*, asks children to identify positive and negative social behaviors through the use of X and O in a tic-tac-toe format. It is important for children to connect their behaviors to their social status. Positive social behaviors increase the likelihood children will make friends and develop peer support (a resiliency factor).

Reproducible Worksheet 9.4, *Being Assertive*, describes the differences between passive, aggressive, and assertive behaviors and gives children the chance to identify each of the three types of responses to various social situations. Assertiveness can help children of incarcerated parents to minimize any anxious or aggressive tendencies they may have learned and to communicate in respectful ways to both themselves and others.

Reproducible Worksheet 9.5, *Problems, Problems, Problems*, acknowledges that from time to time, friendships can be difficult, and problems may need to be addressed. Two social problems are listed and children are asked to come up with three solutions for each problem. Social problem-solving is best learned when children are asked to generate multiple solutions to a problem. Social problem-solving is a valuable social skill as it is associated with prosocial behavior and social competence (Mayeaux & Cillessen, 2003).

Reproducible Worksheet 9.6, *Asking before Acting*, addresses problems of impulsivity in social interactions. It asks children to slow down and consider what they should say before acting. Research tells us individuals who are impulsive have problems in social relationships, which emphasizes the importance of impulse control in making and keeping friends (Landau & Moore, 1991; Patterson & Newman, 1993).

Putting Yourself in Someone Else's Shoes

"Putting yourself in someone else's shoes" is called empathy. Empathy means you can recognize and understand another person's feelings. Think of someone you know. Think about her/his thoughts and feelings. Then write her/his name in the blanks and circle the feeling that best fits what *s/he* would feel (not how *you* would feel).

I wonder how Lisa feels?

1. How would _____ feel if someone called her/him "Stupid?"
   - a. Angry
   - b. Sad
   - c. Embarrassed
   - d. Upset

2. How would _____ feel if s/he found out s/he had to give a speech in front of the whole school?
   - a. Excited
   - b. Terrified
   - c. Nervous
   - d. Confused

3. How would _____ feel if s/he made 100% on a spelling test?
   - a. Relaxed
   - b. Proud
   - c. Happy
   - d. Surprised

4. How would _____ feel if her/his grandmother just got put into the hospital?
   - a. Angry
   - b. Sad
   - c. Worried
   - d. Hopeless

5. How would _____ feel if s/he sat in chocolate?
   - a. Silly
   - b. Embarrassed
   - c. Angry
   - d. Careless

Showing an Interest in Others

Making friends means you know how to show an interest in what others like. That means you need to talk about what they like to do. Look at the pictures below. Each child is doing something. In the speech bubbles next to each child, write down what you would say or ask in order to show you were interested in her/him and the things s/he does.

Social Skills Tic-Tac-Toe

There are behaviors that will lose friends, and there are behaviors that will make and keep friends. Put an O over the statements that describe behaviors with good social skills (i.e., good ways to make and keep friends) and put an X over the statements with poor social skills (i.e., ways to lose friends and keep kids away). How many tic-tac-toes do you get?

Congratulating a classmate who won an art contest	**Waiting for a classmate to finish getting a drink of water before going to lunch**	**Complaining about a teammate who missed a goal during soccer**
Laughing at someone when they give a wrong answer	**Inviting the new kid to play with you at recess**	**Saying you are bored when at a friend's house**
Looking grumpy while walking down the hall	**Saying, "Nice shot!" to a classmate who just made a basket**	**Saying "Hi" to people in the hallway**

Being Assertive

Being *assertive* means you know how to express your thoughts and feelings in a firm, self-confident way. It is different from being *passive*, which is giving in to others, and it is different from being *aggressive*, which is being forceful with others. Below are some situations that have several responses. In each situation, circle the *assertive* response and put an X over the *passive* and *aggressive* responses.

Charlene and Maria have been having a conflict over a shirt Charlene borrowed from Maria. When Charlene returned it, it had a stain on it that it didn't have before Maria loaned it to her.

1. Maria just forgets about it.
2. Maria yells at Charlene and calls her names.
3. Maria asks Charlene to do something about the stain.

Javier and Carl are sitting next to each other at lunch, and Javier is eating with his mouth open. It is really getting on Carl's nerves.

1. Carl kicks Javier under the table.
2. Carl asks Javier politely to please keep his mouth closed while chewing.
3. Carl ignores it.

Brittany and Jan want to play a board game and Brittany has said she wants to go first. Jan feels like Brittany always goes first when they play something together.

1. Jan tells Brittany she would like to go first this time.
2. Jan whines and says under her breath, "I wanted to go first."
3. Jan knocks the game board over and says she refuses to play if Brittany has to go first.

Hunter made fun of LaVell's shoes because he didn't think they were as cool as his.

1. LaVell beats up Hunter after school.
2. LaVell tells Hunter he doesn't appreciate his comments.
3. LaVell hides and cries.

Jason knocked Chase out of the way so he could be first in line.

1. Chase goes to the back of the line.
2. Chase pushes him back.
3. Chase tells Jason it is not OK to push to the front of the line.

Problems, Problems, Problems

Once in awhile friendships can be difficult. Sometimes friends have problems. This is normal! Good friends learn to be good problem-solvers. Good problem-solvers know how to come up with lots of solutions for a problem. There are two problems listed below with lines drawn to circles. Write down three solutions to each problem in the circles at the end of the lines.

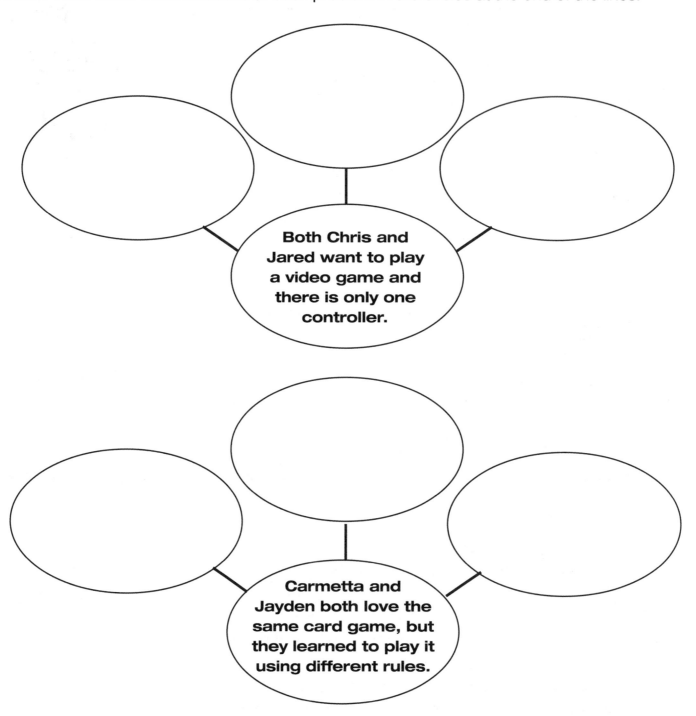

Both Chris and Jared want to play a video game and there is only one controller.

Carmetta and Jayden both love the same card game, but they learned to play it using different rules.

Asking Before Acting

Sometimes kids act before thinking about what they should say first. Acting too quickly without asking permission can cause other kids to feel angry with you – not a good way to make friends! Look at each of the situations below, and inside each speech bubble, write down what you should say before acting.

Your friends have built a fort, and you would like to go in. Before going in, what do you need to ask them?

```
_____
_____
_____
```

You would like to borrow your classmate's red marker. Before taking it, what do you need to ask him?

```
_____
_____
_____
```

You would like to join in a game of basketball. Before joining in, what do you need to ask?

```
_____
_____
_____
```

Lesson 10
Planning for the Future

Notes to Facilitator

Research has begun to recognize that a future orientation is an important resiliency factor for low-income, highly-stressed minority youth (McCabe & Barnett, 2000; Wyman, Cowen, Work, Raoof, Gribble, Parker, & Wannon, 1992). It has been associated with fewer conduct problems (Dubow et al., 2001; Quinton, Pickles, Maughan, & Rutter, 1993), positive social-emotional adjustment (Wyman, Cowen, Work, & Kerley, 1993), higher levels of school involvement (Dubow et al., 2001), and reduced teen pregnancy (Schwab-Zabin & Hayward, 1993). Having a future orientation means children have expectations, goals, hope, and aspirations directing their current behavior. Indeed, having a future orientation means having a positive outlook on the future and having confidence in one's ability to overcome the challenges that are inherent in reaching one's goals.

Unfortunately, many children of incarcerated parents develop a dispositional or defensive pessimism regarding their future. Due to ongoing trauma and shame, they may not have any sense of future, or they may only see a future of disappointment. Research shows children with low levels of hope about the future have more externalizing and internalizing problems - even after social support and stress are controlled for (Hagen, Myers, & Mackintosh, 2005). Given that a positive future orientation acts as an important protective factor in the midst of multiple psychosocial stressors, enhancing future thinking, planning, and hope is crucial for children of incarcerated parents.

Research shows that a positive expectation for the future develops from high levels of family support, stable school connections and strong problem-solving abilities (Dubow et al., 2001; Yowell, 2000). In addition, a positive future orientation includes elements of optimism, realism, and internal locus of control.

» **Optimism**
Optimism is the confidence positive things can happen. Optimistic individuals see adversities simply as temporary setbacks and compartmentalize them to specific situations instead of generalizing problems to other areas of life. Optimism is needed to move beyond frustration and to assume one's goals can and will be met.

> **Research shows that a positive expectation for the future develops from high levels of family support, stable school connections and strong problem-solving abilities.**

» **Realism**
Optimism also needs to be balanced with realism. Unrealistic optimism may set children up for repeated failure and hopelessness. Realistic goals are those where there is an understanding of the necessary preparation as well as accessibility to the resources needed to accomplish the goals.

» **Internal locus of control**
Internal locus of control is the belief a person can determine his/her own future outcomes. Children with an internal locus of control believe they have a large amount of control over their own accomplishments or failures (as opposed to children with an external locus of control who believe external forces - like luck or other people - have control over their accomplishments or failures). McCabe and Barnett (2000) found that kinship social support contributes to an internal locus of control for African American youth.

There are many socializing agents for future orientation, such as parents, extended family members, teachers, peers, mentors, etc. While cognitive development may influence the ability to realistically conceptualize the future, assisting children of incarcerated parents in developing daily, weekly, and future aspirations and goals is an important treatment objective.

Suggestions:

» Encourage parents and extended family members to frequently verbalize support for children's realistic dreams and goals. Research shows family support directly influences children's optimism about the future (McCabe & Barnett, 2000). In the absence of substantial family support, teachers, mentors, ministers, and peers can also provide reinforcement for children's dreams and goals.

» Develop strategies and possibilities for children to experience success. Help them to identify the internal qualities that contributed to those successes. Help them get in touch with their own sense of pride in those accomplishments (e.g., "Aren't you proud of yourself for doing that?").

» Emphasize and give choices whenever possible. This will help to develop an internal locus of control and a sense of empowerment.

» Help children set goals for themselves each week/month/year.

» Encourage children to save money for a particular goal. Help them open savings accounts, when possible.

» Teach and talk about the concept of delayed gratification.

» Teach children how to reframe events in a positive light. For example, if something negative happens or failure occurs, help then to say "I didn't do well on that spelling test, but it's a good thing there are several more that I can do well on to bring up my grade" or "That idea didn't work, but at least I know what to do next time."

» Make books available from the library about various careers.

» Discuss the employment opportunities available within and around the child's community. Moreover, discuss the strategies needed in order to attain those jobs.

Script

The decisions you make today affect the kind of person you will be tomorrow. It is important for you to start thinking about your future and the kind of person you want to be. People who are optimistic (or believe good things will happen to them) usually have more happy feelings and better experiences. It is important to have realistic dreams for the future and to identify ways your dreams can come true. For example, if you dream of playing high school basketball, you can reach this goal by starting to practice playing basketball now. If you want to be a doctor some day, you will have to know a lot about science, and you should pay extra attention in science class now. Making plans for the future is an important part of having a successful life.

Prison Letters

Dear Son,

I have been away from home for a long time now. I still miss you every minute. I have good news. I got to go to school here. I am getting ready to take my GED, and then I will even get to take some college classes in business. That means if I ever get out of here, I might be able to find a good job. The caseworker here said he can even help me find a place to work when that day comes. I still don't know when I might be able to come home, but no matter what, I will not lose hope. I wanted to thank you for continuing to write me letters. It means so much to me that you have let me continue to feel like I am a part of your life even while I am away.

Love you always,
Dad

Dear Dad,

Now I am the one who is proud of you! That is great that you are going to be a college student. Now when my friends ask where you are, I can say you are away at school. Just kidding! Ms. Wells is helping me apply for a special art camp this summer. She says I have real talent. She says after this art camp, the kids sell their artwork for like a hundred dollars or something! Can you believe it? I am going to be a real artist! I am starting to believe that no matter what, everything is going to be ok. I know now I am a strong person. I am glad I have a family that loves me, even if my family is a little different from most of my friends' families. I think it is OK to be different. I hope we will all be together again soon.

Love you a whole bunch,

Big Al (that is my new nickname)

Questions:

1. Why is it important to have hope?

2. What do you think will be in store for Alonzo in the future?

3. What would you like to do in the future?

4. What have you learned from Alonzo and his dad?

Additional Discussion Questions

» Why is it helpful to think about the future?

» What is something you might like to be when you grow up? What are some things you would have to do in order to be that?

» If you were going to write a book about your life, name 3 chapters.

» What is something you think you would be good at but haven't had the chance to try?

» What do you think is a good age to start a family of your own?

Activities

{Taking Steps Towards my Goal}

Objective: To identify goals and steps it will take to reach those goals

Have the child draw a picture of a goal s/he has for the next year, such as getting better grades, getting along with my sister, playing football, etc. Put this picture on the floor several feet away from the child. Then have the child walk towards the goal but with each step, s/he must name something s/he has to do to get to the goal (e.g., for good grades, s/he asks for help, does homework every night, etc.).

For group activity, have the children share their goals with the group and then take turns putting their goals on the floor and walking towards them. Allow group members to help think of steps if anyone gets stuck.

Follow-up: Ask the child(ren) if they know of anyone who has set goals for her/himself. What was her/his goal and how did s/he achieve it? Have the child(ren) identify why it is important to set goals.

{My Dream House}

Objective: To think about the future and consider a plan

Provide child with art supplies, such as a large piece of paper, markers, etc. Tell him/her to imagine the house s/he will live in when s/he grows up.

For group activity, have kids pair up. Each child should choose two markers and his/her partner should choose two markers that are different colors. Have each pair design a house – they must use about the same amount of each color on the house, and each person can only draw with the markers s/he personally chose. Explain that part of being successful in life is learning to work together with others.

Follow-up: Ask the child(ren) to identify things it will take in order to buy this house (e.g., job, education, savings).

{When I Grow Up}

Objective: To promote future-oriented thinking

Ask the child to identify what s/he want to be when s/he grows up. Help the child research this profession online and make a list of what s/he will need to accomplish in order to reach this goal.

For example, a professional football player will need to be fit, lift weights, play high school football, learn sportsmanship, get into college to play college ball, have a back up plan, etc. A doctor will have to do well in science and math, be a good listener, go to college and more college, etc. Have the child identify a few things s/he needs to do now to prepare for this future, and draw a picture of him/her accomplishing the goal.

For group activity, have the kids take turns researching their different professions or have them do this as homework. Have each person tell the group about what s/he found out.

Follow-up: Discuss if there was anything that surprised the child(ren) about what was needed in order to do what s/he wants as an adult. Ask the child(ren) if there is anything that s/he could work on now in order to achieve this goal.

{The Optimistic Story}
Objective: To develop positive thinking

Part of being successful is having an optimistic attitude, which means expecting and looking for good things to happen. Start a story with "Once upon a time …" Have the child create something good that happens next in the story. The facilitator will then say something bad happens. The child will again create the next sentence with a more positive turn of events. Let this go on for about 10 turns each, and let the child end on a positive note.

For group activity, have one child start the story "Once upon a time …" The next child says something bad happens (e.g., "Once upon a time, Johnny was upset because he couldn't play outside."). The next child offers a sentence describing a more positive turn of events (e.g., "The good thing was he had an indoor swimming pool!"). The next child then introduces a negative idea, and so on. Let the story go on for at least five minutes. After five minutes, the last player comes up with a positive ending to the story.

Follow-up: Ask the child(ren) how it felt to identify positive aspects of the story. Discuss why it might be helpful to think more positively.

{Opportunity Quote}
Objective: To focus on finding opportunities in the midst of difficult times

Explain to the child what the definitions of optimism and pessimism are (i.e. thinking on the bright side and thinking on the dark side of situations). Write the following quotation by Winston Churchill on a dry erase board: "*A pessimist sees the difficulty in every opportunity; an optimist sees the opportunity in every difficulty.*" Ask the child to discuss its meaning and how s/he might apply it to a personal difficulty.

For group activity, have the children share their thoughts and ideas about the quotation with the group and then take turns sharing a personal difficulty they would like to apply it to.

Follow-up: Ask the child(ren) if s/he can think of any examples from history or from the media or from the lives of people s/he knows of those who have turned difficulty into opportunity (i.e. Oprah Winfrey who lived in poverty and was abused as a child but grew up to one of America's most influential people).

{What will I be like?}
Objective: To visualize future-selves and promote future-oriented thinking

Give the child several pieces of paper and have him/her draw a picture of what s/he will look like as a teenager, as a college student, as a mom or dad, as a professional, and as a grandparent. On the pictures have him/her make a list of what s/he imagines s/he will do at that age, how s/he will feel, what his/her friends will be like, what s/he will like to do, etc.

For a group activity, children can each draw their own pictures and then share with the group, or have each group member chose one stage of life to imagine (one child does teenager, one does college student, etc.).

Follow-up: Discuss how the child(ren) could learn to be realistically optimistic about his/her future. What kinds of things does s/he need to continually tell her/himself?

Reproducible Worksheets
Reproducible Worksheet 10.1, *Optimism for the Future*, lists several statements children are asked to classify as optimistic or pessimistic. When introducing the concepts of optimism and pessimism, it is useful to clearly differentiate and define optimistic thinking. This allows children to later restructure cognitions to be more positive (optimistic).

Reproducible Worksheet 10.2, *How Optimism and Pessimism Work*, directs children to complete a chart showing them the differences in thoughts, feelings, and actions when one is an optimistic thinker versus when one is a pessimistic thinker.

Reproducible Worksheet 10.3, *Realistic vs. Unrealistic*, introduces children to the idea that not all goals may be realistic based on the children's own strengths and weaknesses. They are asked to examine their own assets and limitations and to identify realistic and unrealistic goals for themselves. While this worksheet is not intended to limit children's potential, it is based on research that shows children in poverty often name unrealistic goals and then are unable to accomplish their aspirations (McCabe & Barnett, 2000).

Reproducible Worksheet 10.4, *Goal Setting*, asks children to identify a goal they have for themselves and to list the action steps needed to accomplish the goal. Goal setting/planning is an effective tool for making progress and accomplishing one's goals. It is an important part of personal development and ensures individuals are clearly aware of what is expected.

Reproducible Worksheet 10.5, *My Possibilities*, helps children to consider several career possibilities. While it is recognized children will change their ideas of "what they want to be when they grow up" many, many times, this worksheet not only assists children in seeing multiple possibilities, but it also helps them connect their own personal attributes to various jobs.

Reproducible Worksheet 10.6, *My Future Relationships*, acknowledges that another part of future orientation is looking forward to partnered relationships. It lists several healthy relationship attributes and asks children to define the terms and give examples of them.

Optimism for the Future

Optimism means having a positive outlook about others, yourself, and the future. It is the opposite of pessimism, which is a *negative* or dark outlook on others, yourself, and the future. People who are optimistic have better health, better relationships, and more enjoyment in life than people who are pessimistic. Look at the statements below. Color the optimistic ones yellow and the pessimistic ones brown.

I am never going to amount to anything.

I'm going to go to the junior college that is nearby.

I have goals for myself!

I am going to be a teacher when I grow up.

I could never be a doctor. Kids in my neighborhood never grow up to be doctors.

I'm probably going to end up in jail, too.

I can see myself with lots of friends in the future.

I can do whatever I set my mind to!

I can't imagine myself with a job.

I will never be able to get a decent paying job.

I have what it takes to be happy and successful.

With all the extra work that I have done this year, I bet I make great grades next year!

I plan to run for student council next year.

I am never going to accomplish anything.

I'm probably not going to make it through high school. It'll be too hard.

I'm probably going to always be poor. It's just the way that it is around here.

I know I have a bright future because I plan to make it that way!

How Optimism and Pessimism Work

Look below to see how optimism and pessimism create different kinds of thinking, feeling and acting. Using the example provided for you, fill in the thoughts, feelings and actions in the empty spaces in the bottom chart. Then answer the questions at the bottom of the page.

Example:

Situation	Attitude	Thoughts	Feelings	Actions
Taking a spelling test	Optimistic	"This might be hard but, if I do my best, I should do ok."	Perhaps a bit nervous, but hopeful and positive	Try my best; stick with it
Taking a spelling test	Pessimistic	"Spelling is too hard for me, so I will probably fail."	Helpless, hopeless and nervous	Give up easily

Now you fill in the empty squares:

Situation	Attitude	Thoughts	Feelings	Actions
Learning how to dive	Optimistic			
Learning how to dive	Pessimistic			

Which kind of thinking helps you feel better? _____

_____

Which kind of thinking helps you to be more successful? _____

_____

Realistic vs. Unrealistic

A realistic goal is something that is doable and possible given a person's strengths and weaknesses; an unrealistic goal is something that might be more of a fantasy and doesn't seriously consider one's strengths and weaknesses. Make a list of your strengths (talents, abilities, personality traits, support systems, etc.). Then name one of your weaknesses. Look at these closely and decide what is realistic and what is not realistic for **YOU.** Then make a list of three realistic goals and one unrealistic goal.

Example: Jaden's strengths are he is strong, he is a good runner, he is good at building things, he makes friends easily, he is tall, and he is good at video games. His weakness is that he is lousy in spelling. Three realistic goals for him are to play on the football team, run for class president, and win a ribbon at the school track meet. One unrealistic goal for him is to win the spelling bee.

Strengths:

_____   _____

_____   _____

_____   _____

Weakness:

_____

Three Realistic Goals:

_____

_____

_____

One Unrealistic Goal:

_____

Goal Setting

Goals are things you want for yourself in the future. They are "targets" you want to "shoot for" by planning and doing. Setting goals for yourself and developing a strategy to achieve those goals is an excellent activity for all of us!

Complete the following:

Write down one of your goals for when you are an adult. Describe what this would be like (e.g., "I want to be an electrician. This would be my full-time job that makes enough money for me to pay all my bills and have extra for fun stuff").

_____

_____

_____

Now write down five (5) specific steps you need to complete before you can accomplish your goal (e.g., for an electrician: finish high school, save money for additional training, enroll at a technical college, attend classes, take certification test, etc.).

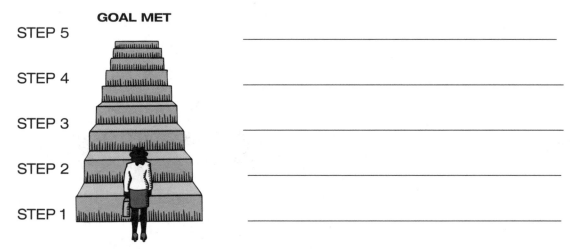

GOAL MET

STEP 5 _____

STEP 4 _____

STEP 3 _____

STEP 2 _____

STEP 1 _____

What obstacle(s) might get in your way (e.g., I hate to do homework, so I may not graduate from high school) and how can you overcome that obstacle (e.g., I could stay after school until my homework is done each day)?

OBSTACLE(S): _____

PLAN TO OVERCOME: _____

My Possibilities

There are several things you could be when you grow up based on your likes and your strengths. Complete the following sentences by writing in a job title and the reason you would be good at that profession.

I could be a _____ because _____

_____ .

I could be a _____ because _____

_____ .

I could be a _____ because _____

_____ .

I could be a _____ because _____

_____ .

I could be a _____ because _____

_____ .

I could be a _____ because _____

_____ .

My Future Relationships

As kids grow up into adults, they often have important relationships with one significant person. These relationships take a lot of work in order to make them healthy. Listed below are some important characteristics of healthy relationships. Write down what you think each of the terms means, and then give an example.

Mutual Respect

Meaning: _____

Example: _____

Trust

Meaning: _____

Example: _____

Good communication

Meaning: _____

Example: _____

Freedom

Meaning: _____

Example: _____

Quality Time between Children and Caregivers – Suggestions from Lesson 2

Play a board game or card game

Give each other a hand or foot massage

Share jokes

Put on some music and dance

Share reading a book

Make up a list of new words and their meanings

Draw a shared picture

Look at old family pictures

Go for a walk

Cook something

Make up a cooperative story

Build something

Play hopscotch or hoola-hoop

Create a garden

Give each other silly hairdos

Dress up as clowns

Make modeling clay and create sculptures

Put on a puppet show

Finger-paint

Blow bubbles

Do a craft together

Create unique 'musical instruments' from the kitchen and play a song

Stop the Stinkin' Thinkin' Game - Lesson 3 Activity

My family is not as good as everyone else's.	I'm not good at anything.	Everyone is thinking bad things about me.
Nobody likes me.	Police are bad people.	My parent will probably die in prison or jail.
Nothing ever goes right in my life.	I am worthless.	My teacher thinks I'm a bad kid.
What happened to my family is all my fault.	My parent is all alone right now.	I am all alone.

Feelings First Aid Kit – Lesson 4 Activity

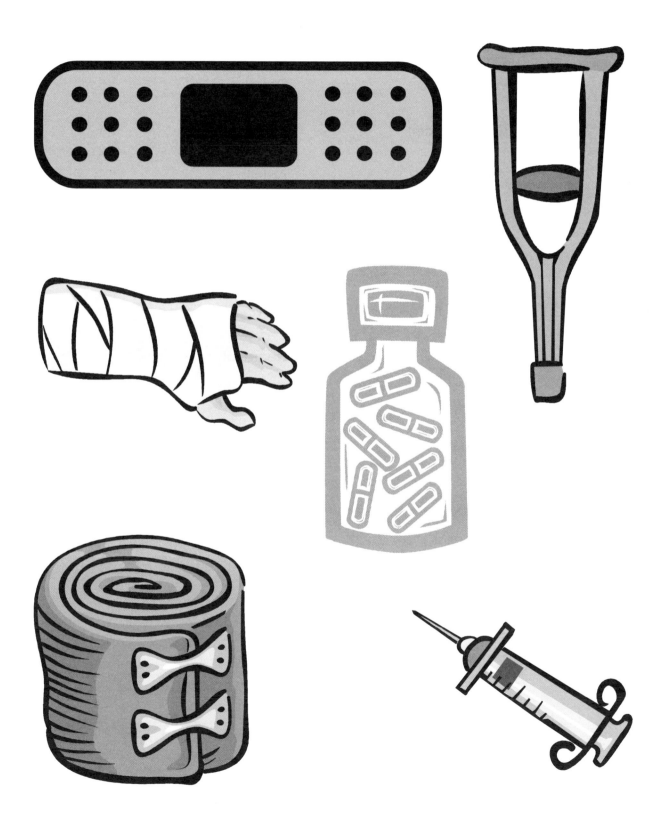

The Person I Miss - Lesson 4 Activity

Loving	Kind	Funny
Nice	Mean	Creative
Strong	Wild	Crazy
Pretty	Good Dancer	Smart
Caring	Annoying	Artistic
Rich	Happy	Angry
Tearful	Difficult	Fantastic
Night Owl	Morning Person	Sick
Healthy	Muscular	Beautiful
Handsome	Hurtful	Magic
Super	Irritable	Athletic
Fast	Lazy	Sad
Magnetic	Wonderful	Cute
Hilarious	Comforting	Joker
Weird	Smelly	Clean

Bag of Tricks – Lesson 7 Activity

Dealing with Anger Scavenger Hunt - Lesson 8 Activity

Name of person you are interviewing:_____

Age _____

Do you ever get angry? ___Yes ___ No

How do you make yourself feel better when you are angry? _____

_____

Do you have any advice for someone who is learning to control their anger?_____

_____

Name of person you are interviewing:_____

Age _____

Do you ever get angry? ___Yes ___ No

How do you make yourself feel better when you are angry? _____

_____

Do you have any advice for someone who is learning to control their anger?_____

_____

Name of person you are interviewing:_____

Age _____

Do you ever get angry? ___Yes ___ No

How do you make yourself feel better when you are angry? _____

_____

Do you have any advice for someone who is learning to control their anger?_____

_____

Name of person you are interviewing:_____

Age _____

Do you ever get angry? ___Yes ___ No

How do you make yourself feel better when you are angry? _____

_____

Do you have any advice for someone who is learning to control their anger?_____

_____

Friendly Behaviors – Lesson 9 Activity

Sharing	Hitting	Name Calling
Giving Compliments	Inviting Someone to Play a Game	Pushing
Hugging	Leaving Someone Out	Tripping
Laughing at Someone who is Hurt	Caring About Others' Feelings	Listening
Smiling	Frowning	Kicking

References

Barrera, M., & Garrison-Jones, C. (1992). Family and peer social support as specific correlates of depressive symptoms. Journal of Abnormal Clinical Psychology, 20(1), 1-16.

Baunach, P. J. (1985). *Mothers in prison.* New Brunswick, NJ: Transaction, Inc.

Beck, E. & Jones, S. (2007). Children of the condemned: Grieving the loss of a father to death row. *Omega, 56*(2), 191-215.

Benard, B. (1991). Fostering resiliency in kids: Protective factors in the family, school, and community (Northwest Regional Educational Laboratory). Portland, OR: Western Center for Drug-Free Schools and Communities.

Bogenschneider, K. (1996). An ecological risk/protective theory for building prevention programs, policies, and community capacity to support youth. *Family Relations, 45,* 127-138.

Bowen, M. (1978). *Family therapy in clinical practice.* New York: Jason Aronson.

Bowen, N.K., & Bowen, G.L. (1998). The mediating role of educational meaning in the relationship between home academic culture and academic performance. *Family Relations, 47,* 45-51.

Bowen, N.K., & Bowen, G.L. (1998). The effects of home microsystem risk factors and school microsystem protective factors on student academic performance and affective investment in schooling. *Social Work in Education, 20,* 219-231.

Caetano, R. & Trocki, R. (2003). Expoxure to Family Violence and Temperament Factors as Predictors of Adult Psychopathology and Substance Use Outcomes. *Journal of Addiction Nursing, 14,* 183-192.

Carnegie, D. (1936). *How to Win Friends and Influence People.* New York: Simon & Schuster.

Carter B., & McGoldrick M. (1989). The changing family life cycle: A framework for family therapy. In: Carter B, McGoldrick M (eds) *The Changing Family Life Cycle: A Framework for Family Therapy,* 2nd ed. Boston, Massachusetts: Ilyn and Bacon, 3-28.

Children of Incarcerated Parents. (Winter, 2007). Virginia Child Protection Newsletter, 81, 1-8.

Cohen, J., Mannarino, A. Murray, L., & Igelman, R. (2006). Psychosocial Interventions for Maltreated and Violence-Exposed Children. *Journal of Social Issues, 62*(4), 737-766.

Cunningham, A. (2001). Forgotten Families: The Impacts of Imprisonment. *Family Matters, 59,* 35-38.

Davidson, K., MacGregor, M.W., Stuhr, J., Dixon, K., & MacLean, D. (2000). Consructive anger verbal behavior predicts blood pressure in a population-based sample. *Health Psychology, 19,* 55-64.

Deffenbacher, J.L., Lynch, R.S., Oetting, E.R., & Kemper, C.C. (1996). Anger reduction in early adolescents. *Journal of Counseling Psychology, 43*(2), 149-157.

Dreyer, P.H. (1994). Designing curriculare identity interventions for secondary schools. In S.L. Archer (Ed.) *Interventions for Adolescent Identity Development* (121-140). Thousand Oaks, Ca.: Sage.

Dubow, E.F., Arnett, M., Smith, K., Ippolito, M.F. (2001). Predictors of future expectations of inner-city children: A 9-month perspective study. *Journal of Early Adolescence, 21*(1), 5-28.

Dubow, E. F., Tisak, J., Causey, D., & Hryshko, A. (1991). A two-year longitudinal study of stressful life events, social support, and social problem-solving skills: Contributions to children's behavioral and academic adjustment. *Child Development, 62,* 583-599.

Edin, K., Nelson, T.J., & Paranal, R. (2004). Fatherhood and incarceration as potential turning points in the criminal careers of unskilled men. In Mary Patillo, David F. Weiman, & Bruce Western (Ed.) *Imprisoning America: The Social Effects of Mass Incarceration.* New York: Russell Sage.

Erikson, E.H. (1968). *Identity: Youth and crisis.* New York: W.W. Norton.

Eysenck, M. W., & Calvo, M. G. (1992). Anxiety and performance: The processing efficiency theory. *Cognition and Emotion, 6*(6), 409-443.

Finn, J. D., Pannozzo, G. M., & Voelkl, K. E. (1995). Disruptive and inattentive-withdrawn behavior and achievement among fourth graders. *Elementary School Journal, 95,* 421-434.

Finn, J. D. & Rock, D.A. (1997). Academic success among students at risk for school failure. *Journal of Applied Psychology, 82*(2), 221-234.

Forbes, D., Phelps, A. J., McHugh, A. F., Debenham, P., Hopwood, M., & Creamer, M. (2004). Imagery rehearsal in the treatment of posttraumatic nightmares in Australian veterans with chronic combat-related PTSD: 12-month follow-up data. *American Journal of Clinical Hypnosis,* Retrieved from http://findarticles.com/p/articles/mi_qa4087/is_/ai_n9424497 on November 25,2008.

Ford, J., & Sutphen, R. D. (1996). Early intervention to improve attendance in elementary school for at-risk children: A pilot program. Social Work in Education, 18, 95-102.

Franz, G. (1995). Stories for therapy: the right story to the right person at the right time. *Contemporary Family Therapy,* 17, 47-64.

Fredericks, J.A., Blumenfeld, P.C., & Paris, A.H. (2004). School engagement: Potential of the concept, state of evidence. *Review of Educational Research, 74*(1), 59-109.

Gabel, S. (1992). Children of incarcerated and criminal parents: Adjustment, behavior, and prognosis. Bulletin of the American Academy of Psychiatry and the Law, 20(1), 33-45.

Goleman, D. (1995). *Emotional intelligence.* New York: Bantam Books.

Greene, S., Haney, C., & Hurtado, A. (2000). Cycles of pain: Risk factors in the lives of incarcerated mothers and their children. *The Prison Journal, 80*(1), 3-23.

Gross, A., Messer, S., and Morris T. (1995). Enhancement of the Social Interaction and Status of Neglected Children: A Peer-Pairing Approach. *Journal of Clinical Child Psychology, 24*(1), 11-20.

Grossman, J.B., & Garry, E.M. (1997). Mentoring: A proven delinquency prevention strategy. Washington, DC: Office of Juvenile Justice and Delinquency Prevention Bulletin.

Grossman, P.B. & Hughes, J.N. (1992). Self-control interventions with internalizing disorders: A review and analysis. *School Psychology Review, 21*(2), 229-245.

Hagen, K.A., Myers, B.J., & Mackintosh, V.H. (2005) Hope, social support, and behavioral problems in at-risk children. *The American Journal of Orthopsychiatry, 75*(2), 211-9.

Hairston, J. C. F. (2002). Prisoners and families: Parenting issues during incarceration. *From Prison to Home, 1, 42-54.*

Harter, S. (1998). The effects of child abuse on the self-system. *Journal of Aggression, Maltreatment and Trauma, 2*(1), 147-169.

Herrera, C., Sipe, C.L., & McClanahan, W.S. (2000). *Mentoring school-age children: Relationship development in community-based and school-based programs* (PDF). Philadelphia: Public Private Ventures. (On-line: cited 23 January 2003).

Johnston, D. (1995). Effects of Parental Incarceration. In *Children of Incarcerated Parents,* edited by Katherine Gabel and Denise Johnston (59–89). New York: Lexington Books.

Johnston, D. (2001). *Incarceration of women and effects on parenting.* Paper prepared for a conference, Effects of Incarceration on Children and Families, sponsored by Northwestern University, Chicago, IL.

Johnson, E., & Waldfogel, J. (2002). Parental incarceration: Recent trends and implications for child welfare. *Social Services Review, 76*(3), 460-479.

Jones, S. & Beck, E. (2007). Disenfranchised grief and nonfinite loss as experienced by the families of death row inmates. *Omega, 54*(4), 281-299.

Jucovy, L. (2003). Amachi: Mentoring children of prisoners in Philadelphia. A publication of Public/Private Ventures: The Center on Research for Religion and Urban Civil Society Retrieved on November 15, 2008 from http://www.ppv.org/ppv/publications/assets/21_publication.pdf

Juvonen, J. (2006). Sense of belonging, social bonds and school functioning. In Patricia Alexander and Philip Winn (Eds.) *Handbook of Educational Psychology.* Mahwah, NJ, US: Lawrence Erlbaum Associates Publishers, 655-674.

Jose-Kampfner, C. (1991), Michigan program makes children's visits meaningful, *Corrections Today,* 130–134.

Kampfner, C. (1995). Post-traumatic stress reactions in children of imprisoned mothers. In K. Gabel & D. Johnston (Eds.), *Children of Incarcerated Parents.* New York: Lexington Books.

Katz, L. (1996). *How Can We Strengthen Children's Self-Esteem.* ERIC Clearinghouse on Elementary and Early Childhood Education. Online at: http://www.kidsource.com/kidsource/content2/strengthen_children_self.html.

Kaufman, K. R. & Kaufman, N. D. (2005). Childhood mourning: Prospective case analysis of multiple losses. *Death Studies, 29, 237-249.*

Kazura, K. (2001). Family programming for incarcerated parents: A needs assessment among inmates. *Journal of Offender Rehabilitation, 32*(4), 67-83.

Klein, S.R., Bartholomew, G.S., & Hibbert, J. (2002). Inmate family functioning. *International Journal of Offender Therapy and Comparative Criminology, 46.*

Landau, S. & Moore, L.A. (1991). Social skill deficits in children with attention deficit hyperactivity disorder. *School Psychology Review, 20, 235-251.*

La Vigne, N.G., Naser, R.L., Brooks, L.E., & Castro, J.L. (2005). Examining the effect of incarceration and in-prison family contact on prisoners' family relationships. *Journal of Contemporary Criminal Justice 21*(4), 314-335.

Lavoie, R. (2008). *The Motivation Breakthrough: 6 Secrets for Turning on the Tuned-Out Child.* New York: Touchstone Books.

Lowenstein, A. (1986). Temporary single parenthood—The case of prisoners' families. *Family Relations, 35, 79-85.*

Marin, K., Bohanek, J., & Fivush, R. (2008). Positive effects of talking about the negative: family narratives of negative experiences and preadolescents' perceived competence. *Journal of Research on Adolescence, 18*(3), 573-593.

Mayeux, L. & Cillessen, A. (2003). Development of social problem solving in early childhood: Stability, change and associations with social competence. *Journal of Genetic Psychology, 164*(2), 153-173.

Mazza, C. (2002). And then the world fell apart: The children of incarcerated fathers. *Families in Society: The Journal of Contemporary Human Services, 83*(5/6), 521-529.

McCabe, K., & Barnett, D. (2000). First comes work, then comes marriage: Future orientation among African American adolescents. *Family Relations, 49*(1), 63-71.

Miller, K. M. (2006). The impact of parental incarceration on children: An emerging need for effective interventions. *Child and Adolescent Social Work Journal, 23*(4), 472-486.

Miller, S., & Coll, E. (2007). From social withdrawal to social confidence: Evidence for possible pathways. *Current Psychology 26*(2), 86-101.

Mumola, C. J. (2000). *Incarcerated parents and their children.* Bureau of Justice Statistics.

Murray, J., Janson, C.G., & Farrington, D.P. (2007). Crime in adult offspring of prisoners: A cross-national comparison of two longitudinal samples. *Criminal Justice and Behavior 34*. 133-149.

Nesmith, A., & Ruhland, E. (2008). Children of incarcerated parents: Challenges and resiliency, in their own words. *Children and Youth Services Review 30*, 1119-1130.

Parke, R.D., & Clarke-Stewart, K.A. (2001). Effects of parental incarceration on young children.Paper presented at *From Prison to Home: The Effects of Incarceration and Reentry on Children, Families and Communities* Conference, Jan. 30-31. Washington, DC: U.S. Department of Health and Human Services.

Patterson, C.M., & Newman, J.P. (1993). Reflectivity and learning from aversive events: Toward a psychological mechanism for the syndromes of disinhibition. *Psychological Review, 100*(4) 716-736.

Pelco, L.E. & Reed-Victor, E. (2007). Self-regulation and learning-related social skills: Intervention ideas for elementary school students. *Preventing School Failure, 51*(3), 36-42.

Phillips, S. D., Burns, B. J., Wagner, H. R., Kramer, T. L., & Robbins, J. M. (2002). Parental incarceration among adolescents receiving mental health services. *Journal of Child and Family Studies, 11*(4), 385-399.

Phillips, S.D., & Gleeson, J.P. (2007).What we Know Now that we Didn't Know Then about the Criminal Justice System's Involvement in Families with whom Child Welfare Agencies have Contact. Findings from a Landmark National Study [Electronic Version]. *Research Brief: Children, Families, and the Criminal Justice System*. Retrieved on December 1, 2008 from http://www.uic.edu/jaddams/college/research/What_we_know_now.pdf.

Quinton, D., Pickles, A., Maughan, B. & Rutter, M. (1993). Partners, peers and pathways: Assortative pairing and continuities and discontinuities in conduct disorder. *Developmental Psychology, 5*, 763-783.

Ray, R.D., Wilhelm, F.H., & Gross, J.J. (2008). All in the mind's eye? Anger rumination and reappraisal. *Journal of Personality and Social Psychology, 94*(1), 133-145.

Richman, J. M., & Bowen, G. L. (1997). School failure: An ecological-interactional-developmental perspective. In M. W. Fraser (Ed.), Risk and resilience in childhood: An ecological perspective (95-116). Washington, DC: NASW Press.

Sack, W.H., Seidler, J., & Thomas, S. (1976). The children of imprisoned parentes: A psychosocial exploration. *American Journal of Orthopsychiatry, 46*(4), 618-628.

Schwab-Zabin, L. & Hayward, S.C. (1993). *Adolescent Sexual Behavior and Childbearing*. Newbury Park, Ca.: Sage Publications.

Simmons, (2000). Report from the California Research Bureau. *Children of Incarcerated Parents*. Retrieved September 15, 2008 from http://www.library.ca.gov/crb/00/notes/V7N2.pdf.

Snell, T. L. (1994). *Women in prison*. Bureau of Justice Statistics.

Snyder-Joy, Z. & Carlo, T. (1998). Parenting through prison walls: Incarcerated mothers and child visitation. In S. Miller (Ed.), *Crime Control and Women*. Newbury Park, CA: Sage Publications, Inc.

Springer, D., Lynch, C., & Rubin, A. (2000). Effects of a solution-focused mutual aid group for Hispanic children of incarcerated parents. *Child and Adolescent Social Work Journal, 17*(6), 431-441.

Stanton, A. M. (1980). *When mothers go to jail*. New York: Lexington Books.

Stein, B. D., Jaycox, L. H., Kataoka, S., Rhodes, H. J., & Vestal, K. D. (2003). Prevalence of child and adolescent exposure to community violence. *Clinical Child and Family Psychology Review, 6*(4), 247–264.

Travis, J. (2004). Reentry and reintegration.: New perspectives on the challenges of mass incarceration. In P. Patillo, D. Weiman, & B. Western (Eds.). *Imprisoning America: The Social Effects of Mass Incarceration* (46-75). New York: Russell Sage Foundation.

Travis, J. (2005). *But they all come back: Facing the challenges of prisoner reentry*. Washington, DC: Urban Institute Press.

Trzcinski, E., Satyanathan, D., & Ferro, L. (2002). What about me? Children with incarcerated parents. *Michigan Family Impact Seminars*. Briefing Report No. 2002-1.

Wyman, P.A., Cowen, E.L., Work, W.C., & Kerley, J.H. (1993). The role of children's future expectations in self-system functioning and adjustment to life stress: A prospective study of urban at-risk children. *Development and Psychopathology, 5*, 649-661.

Wyman, P.A., Cowen, E.L., Work, W.C. Raoof, B.A., Gribble, P.A., Parker, G.R. & Wannon, M. (1992). Interviews with children who experienced major life stress: family and child attributes that predict resilient outcomes. *Journal of the American Academy of Child and Adolescent Psychiatry, 31*, 904-910.

Yowell, C.M. (2000). Possible selves and future orientation: Exploring hopes and fears of Latino boys and girls. *Journal of Early Adolescence, 20*(3), 245-280.

Zigler, E., Taussig, C., & Black, K. (1992). Early childhood intervention. *American Psychologist, 47*, 997-1006.